THE SECRET LIFE OF TARTAN

THE SECRET LIFE OF TARTAN

How a cloth shaped a nation

VIXY RAE

BLACK & WHITE PUBLISHING

First published in the UK in 2019
This edition first published in 2023 by
Black & White Publishing Ltd
Nautical House, 104 Commercial Street,
Edinburgh, EH6 6NF

A division of Bonnier Books UK
4th Floor, Victoria House, Bloomsbury Square, London, WC1B 4DA
Owned by Bonnier Books
Sveavägen 56, Stockholm, Sweden

A CIP catalogue record is available from the British Library.

ISBN: 978 1 78530 520 7

1 3 5 7 9 10 8 6 4 2

Layout by Black & White
Printed and bound in China

www.blackandwhitepublishing.com

CONTENTS

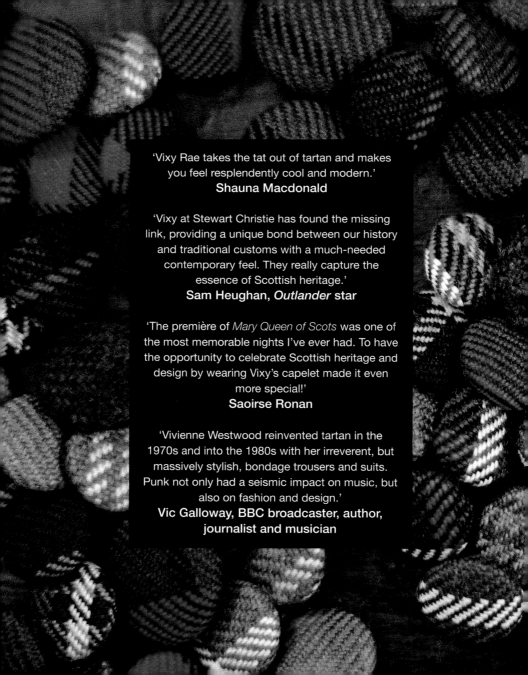

'Vixy Rae takes the tat out of tartan and makes you feel resplendently cool and modern.'
Shauna Macdonald

'Vixy at Stewart Christie has found the missing link, providing a unique bond between our history and traditional customs with a much-needed contemporary feel. They really capture the essence of Scottish heritage.'
Sam Heughan, *Outlander* star

'The première of *Mary Queen of Scots* was one of the most memorable nights I've ever had. To have the opportunity to celebrate Scottish heritage and design by wearing Vixy's capelet made it even more special!'
Saoirse Ronan

'Vivienne Westwood reinvented tartan in the 1970s and into the 1980s with her irreverent, but massively stylish, bondage trousers and suits. Punk not only had a seismic impact on music, but also on fashion and design.'
Vic Galloway, BBC broadcaster, author, journalist and musician

Dedicated to my ray of sunshine:

Saul Mann Rae (MacRae)

FOREWORD

Eric Musgrave in cashmere
'Wispy' scarf in Yellow Stewart tartan
by Begg & Co of Ayr

Christine was a nice girl who worked in a baker's shop in Leeds. Our innocent teenage romance was quite short, but it was slightly prolonged because I was not prepared to make the break until I had retrieved from her possession my extra-long scarf in Royal Stewart tartan.

While this unchivalrous behaviour reflects badly on my spotty self, it underlines the powerful affection tartan can stir even in a Sassenach heart. I loved that scarf. My sister Sue, usefully enough, was studying at fashion college and I persuaded her to sew a few pieces of tartan together to create a five-foot-long muffler in the vividly coloured check.

My connection to the pleasures of tartan was made via Roderick David Stewart, a Londoner who wished he was Scottish. The cover of the 1974 album *Smiler* by Rod Stewart (for it is he of whom I speak) had Our Hero in an alarming satin ensemble against a background of Royal Stewart tartan. Rod the Mod's fascination with his Scottish father's heritage is merely one example of the potent power of Scotland's mythical cloth.

The scarf was no passing fancy (unlike Christine). When in the early 1980s I got my first serious job in journalism, on the trade title *Drapers Record* (later *Drapers*), I forsook saving for a deposit on a flat to have made by a Soho tailor a cracking pair of trousers in the vibrant Buchanan tartan. Why? Because I was worth it, and I like wearing things that other people do not wear.

Shrugging off regular catcalls of 'You look like Rupert Bear!' (like it was a bad thing), I discovered such a richly coloured pattern was very versatile. Really, it went with nothing, so in my eyes it went with everything.

Along the way, I picked up tartan ties, bow ties and scarves, as well as shirts (but were those checks genuine tartans or just, well, checks?).

Later, when attending lots of black-tie dinners became part of my job, I acquired a handsome Black Watch tartan tuxedo. With age came subtlety, but that dark, mysterious pattern still allows me to stand out from the crowd of penguins.

Ringing the changes for my round of corporate junkets, I invested in a pair of bespoke Mitchell tartan trews from a clever man in Dundee called Grant Mitchell. Done in a correct military style, these remain a favourite in the extensive Musgrave wardrobe.

My tartan apogee came in 2014 when I attended an awards dinner for *Drapers*, which by then I was editing, in full Highland dress complete with the kilt in a restrained grey tartan. It was an experience at once exciting, liberating and empowering. The kilt appears to endow the wearer with superpowers – or at least super belief in himself.

So, my relationship with this most intriguing and beguiling of cloths has many facets and is ongoing. You will, I am sure, find my creative friend Vixy Rae's examination of *The Secret Life of Tartan* every bit as inspiring as I have.

Eric Musgrave
Author of *Sharp Suits: a celebration of men's tailoring*

A NOTE FROM THE AUTHOR

As a child of Edinburgh, I couldn't avoid tartan. But I never took it to my heart. I've always had a deep love of colour, which, as my taste and style refined, extended to all other fabrics – from streetwear canvas, bold prints and denims, to respectable hand-loomed tweeds and woollens – but never quite to tartan.

Then I became owner of the oldest bespoke tailors in Scotland and was thrust into an unknown world of formal attire with its remarkable, prestigious heritage, of which the patterns and history of tartan are a cornerstone.

Now I'm finding that tartan encapsulates a deep-rooted pride passed from generation to generation. This strong sense of unity and rebellion came to me, unexpected. This book has been my voyage of discovery to unpick the truth from the myth, the reality from the romance, to understand how a cloth can define a nation. It celebrates the people I'm fortunate enough to have met on my tartan travels and those who have a wealth of knowledge in my cloth-based industry. This marks the start of my personal journey, beyond the shortbread tin . . .

Vixy Rae

AFORE

TARTAN

Glenorchy

Rep green
Rep red
Rep blue

TO LOVE OR TO LOATHE?

For me to start this journey into the secret life of tartan was a complex undertaking. As I grew up in the Edinburgh of the late 1970s and early 1980s, it was clear even to my childish eyes that tartan had become a pastiche parody of itself. The sight of elderly ladies pushing tartan-clad shopping buggies, combined with the ongoing hangover from the Bay City Rollers and Rod Stewart must have played their part. I was fractionally too young to be involved in or influenced by the anarchy of the original punk movement, and so my earliest and least fond memories of tartan are ones which have stuck with me.

On the other hand, my life has always been influenced by colour, so I wonder if the regimented form of the cloth repelled me. I prefer life to be a blurred rainbow of blended colour and texture, and so perhaps the notion of something so defined in its organisation of colour on fabric led me to rebel, and fiercely, against the whole idea. Looking back, my wardrobe was a tartan-free zone up until recent years, and even then I wore it only very cautiously, feeling something of a fraud for my instinctive dislike of it.

But now – at last! – I understand the whole allure of tartan; the irresistible pull that compels its wearers to use it to define, stand out and in some cases shock.

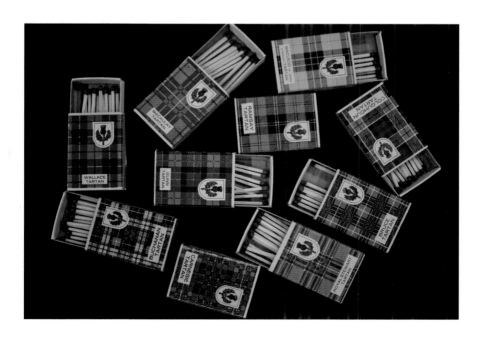

FOR THE LOVE OF TWEED

Admittedly, when it comes to cloth, my first love was always tweed. But the truth is I've realised just how incredible the connection between the two is: how closely linked tartan and tweed are, how their paths cross and intertwine. Throughout history and through many designer collections the two cloths work together and against each other to create ideas of robustness and unity.

There is something very honest about tweed. It is rough and tough; its colours reflect the land. It does exactly what it sets out to do: it owns its truth, uncomplicated and unabashed. And today tweed has returned to vogue. Whether you are a country gamekeeper or an urban hipster, there is no doubt that the cloth speaks of refinement; it is accepted across the range of social interactions.

Looking at tweed and tartan in relation to each other, my deep-down feeling is that tartan is a little less than honest. Where tweed is muted and uses the natural colours of peat, heather, gorse taken from the land, tartan is the opposite. It is more dramatic, and it shouts. Admittedly there are 'loud' tweeds and these can cross the taste boundary. But they also bridge the gap between the hard-working, honest and straightforward cloth of tweed, and its distant, flashier cousin who rebels, shouts and shocks.

Like any trend, everything moves in cycles. Being involved in clothing for most of my working life, I have seen a fair amount of changes. What one generation loves the next hates and the subsequent generation 're-discovers' and 're-invents'. During my early life, tartan had taken on a difficult identity in popular culture. It seemed to be going through a confused and contradictory phase. To a teen in the 1980s – and a Scottish teen at that – it was a hard sell. Fortunately, the direction that tartan has taken in the last two decades has helped define Scotland, but in a fresh, complete and wholesome way. The aesthetics are a lot more pleasing now than they were when I was younger.

FEAR THE FABRIC . . .

I remember flicking through a dog-eared copy of the *Jackie Annual* in an Oxfam shop, while being dragged round by my mother – then a very definite hippy. The photos of the tartan-clad Bay City Rollers intrigued me and repulsed me. Their look was old news as far as I was concerned; it belonged to another generation. And, as a resident of Edinburgh, Scotland's capital city, the loud-mouthed tartan of the Bay City Rollers piled on to the brash selection of tourist fodder on the Royal Mile to give what you might call a bad impression. In my mind, the significance of tartan was not a positive one.

It was a tricky issue for me to deal with. Punk had a presence in the press and the country was in political turmoil (then again when isn't it!). On the one hand, tartan sang a mindless 'Shang-a-Lang' song; on the other, I was told it was all 'Anarchy in the UK'. For me, at this time, it was easier to dismiss tartan altogether; it was best left to the tourists, the punks and the ageing glam rockers.

But what goes around comes around and so, in recent years, that same popular culture has led to a true tartan renaissance. As a fabric known the world over for its distinct pattern and use of colour, it does so much more than just shout 'Scotland!' Tartan's international presence conjures up all the connotations associated with the nation – from unity and kinship, to rebellion and pride, from the cosy bothy to the wild dramatic Highland Glens. These ideas come together to form a more complete and defined image than the one I was raised with.

The girls all love a tartan kilt,
Auld Scotlands greatest pride,
But its not the Kilt itself
. . . . girls love,
Its the bonny lad inside.

CALL IT WHAT YOU WILL . . .

So, what's in a name? Scholars agree that ideas behind the origin of the word 'tartan' vary greatly; there is no fixed answer. '*Tartarin*' was the French word for a coarsely woven cloth of blended wool and linen. Then there is '*tiritaña*' from the Old Spanish – it's the word for a silk fabric, from '*tiritar*' meaning to rustle.

I prefer the Gaelic claim, coming from the words 'tuar' meaning 'colour', and 'tan' meaning 'district', matched with 'tarsainn' meaning 'across'. This beautifully supports the theory that from early times the cloth was a recognition of region rather than clanship. Unfortunately, there is no documentary evidence to support this evocative claim.

THE FIRST TARTAN – OR A TWEED?

However, there is no doubt the origins of the cloth can be found in prehistoric cultures. Some scholars argue that there is mention of tartan in the Bible and claim historical references from tribes from Central Asia. The earliest surviving sample in Scotland has been dated to around the third century AD. It was excavated at the Antonine Wall, a boundary erected by the Romans to keep out the barbarians, near Falkirk. The cloth had been used as a stopper in the top of a jar which contained a cache of Roman coins, so much more about the fabric is unknown. The piece is only small, so the pattern is visible but the bigger picture – or 'swatch'; that is, enough of the fabric to show the look of the whole – can't be seen, so experts have needed to make certain assumptions as to the original pattern. Then there is the debate as to whether it is in fact tartan or – shock, horror – a tweed!

There is little doubt on these shores that the Celts were the first people to become skilled at weaving. This skill was partly to do with the creation of a 'legal' system, the imperative of which was simply to establish a hierarchy. Stripes in cloth were originally there to show social status. The equation was a simple one: the more important you were,

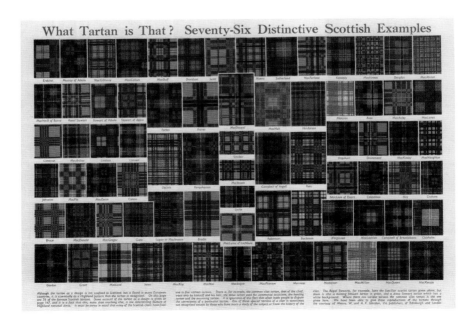

the more stripes you were entitled to. For example, a Celtic king was powerful enough to wear seven stripes, a Druid six and so on. Peasants were granted only a single stripe.

The reason we know all this is because the Romans who invaded the British Isles were in the habit of recording their exploits. Their records show that they recognised the Celts were well versed in the ways of spinning and dyeing yarn; they also make reference to the use of colour in their weaving. In some respects, it appears that Roman weaving techniques reached a high level of mechanical perfection in these ancient times. Their looms were fitted with an elaborate system of 'leashes' or 'heddles' for working out designs mechanically.

As Scotland continued to be invaded from the north and the south, this striped cloth was adopted by those invaders. It seems it wasn't just the cloth but the style of clothing which the marauders embraced too. It was only a matter of time before Scots adopted more modern weaving techniques and so patterns could be woven into the weft, across the fabric. Given that the tunic was, for centuries, the accepted form of masculine dress, it doesn't take much to imagine how this evolved into the kilt as we know it today.

TARTAN AND TWEED TOGETHER

It seems that back in the distant past, the cloth we call tartan was closer to tweed than its modern-day slick cousin. With this in mind, I now find myself able to forgive tartan

for all its past indiscretions, its fakery and brashness. More than forgive, I can embrace it. This new warmth surely stems from the story of its origins, a story which sets it on a journey to become one of the most distinctive and far-reaching cloths in history. Tartan started out as tweed, but of course even tweed wasn't really tweed. Tweed was simply the romantic name for 'tweel', a coarse cloth woven for working clothes. It was a mill clerk's handwriting scrawl which gave rise to this happy quirk of fate; 'tweed' conjured up images of the River Tweed, the countryside and hills, so the name settled and it all fell into place from there.

COLOURS OF THE LAND

The cloth woven by the early Scots was heavy coarse yarn and its colours were taken from the land round and about where its weavers made their homes. Natural dyes were created from lichens, berries, seaweeds, bark, rock and minerals that were gathered in the locality – the colours of these cloths were defined by the area in which they almost literally grew, rather being attached to a particular family.

This is how we can think of the district tartans – such as the Lennox tartan. Lennox or *Leamhnachd* was a significant area of Scotland encompassing Dunbartonshire stretching from the north-eastern shores of Loch Lomond to near Stirlingshire during the Middle Ages. It could possibly be one of the truest representations of tartan from early times, in sett – that is, the square pattern of the cloth – if not in colour.

LIES, LIES, I TELL THEE . . .

This draws me to one of the biggest secrets (or lies) that tartan ever told, and there are a few. After the final Jacobite rebellion, there followed a period in Scottish history when tartan was supposedly banned. The Dress Act of 1746 held the details of the ban, which specifically set out to control the potential for another uprising against the English crown. But as time passed and generations passed, political divisions shifted and the tartan as we know it today was created. It was all down to the idea of one man. This man was Sir Walter Scott. He was responsible for the 'second coming' of tartan, moving it from a Scottish family relic to the height of Hanoverian fashion.

So, when you unravel it, modern tartan is less of a lie and more of a spin: one of the biggest and best PR twists in history. To unite a nation, it was decided that King George IV should visit the Scottish capital as part of a 'grand tour' – the first visit of a reigning monarch in nigh on two centuries. The showstopper would be a gathering of all the clan chieftains to welcome the monarch in a historic pageant. This pageant was envisaged to be as much of a display of Scottish unity as of colour, pomp and ceremony for King George. There was just one problem, and that was the ban. It had been repealed in 1782, but even now, in 1822, there were many who didn't know what their own clan tartan was or even what it looked like.

One of my favourite stories is from the now sadly closed William Wilson & Son mill.

They continued to weave tartan throughout the ban, as the act of proscription did not extend to ladies, children, gentry or nobility. In the early 19th century Wilson's had the best archive in the country. As the time of the pageant drew closer, they received letter after letter from clan chieftains asking what their tartan was and, if they couldn't find the answer in their archives, could the mill please pick one for them! To be caught without one's own tartan for such a landmark social event was unimaginable.

Tartan's history *is* a secretive one – much is folklore, much is myth, and there's an awful lot of Georgian and Victorian romanticism in the mix too. On the other hand, heritage and lineage have kept tartan alive as a vital, present part of Scotland's culture.

Q&A: PETER MACDONALD
Tartan historian

Peter MacDonald is a man who quite possibly has forgotten more than I will ever begin to know about tartan. Peter is Scotland's foremost tartan historian; his main area of interest is the Jacobite era and the early commercial production of tartan. And so, in my quest to weave together the whole historical pattern that is tartan, I turned to him as surely the world's leading authority on its history and its design. I posed a few questions to help ease myself into this new, intricate world of structure and colour, hoping to broaden my knowledge by absorbing some of his. I came away from our meeting convinced that if you were to cut him in half, he would be tartan all the way through – like a stick of rock, only more stylish.

Vixy Rae: How would you define tartan? What is its defining quality?

Peter MacDonald: Historically, the term tartan was used to describe a type of cloth, irrespective of pattern. More commonly, it describes the multi-coloured, cross-barred pattern woven from solid coloured yarns, which distinguishes it from tweed. As a design, tartan is not unique to Scotland but only here did it develop the cultural significance that is inextricably linked to the Highland clans and which later became perhaps the unifying symbol of Scottishness. It is the Fabric of the Nation.

For you, which tartan represents the pinnacle of design in colour and complexity of sett?

There are a number of contenders for the title but perhaps the finest example is the tartan designed in 1713 for the Royal Company of Archers' first uniform. The tartan was replaced by the Black Watch tartan in the late 18th century but not before it had been used as the basis for Ogilvie and Drummond of Strathallan tartans.

And which is your least favourite?

I'm not a fan of a lot of modern fashion tartans, principally because they often use colours and colour combinations that are non-traditional; for example: pink, yellow, purple and light blue, which I just don't find pleasing. I also find the current trend for dull and bland colours, such as those of the Outlander range of tartan, visually unsatisfying and historically misleading.

In the 18th century, red was the colour of choice for those that could afford it, the gentry were invariably painted in red-based tartans and the majority of surviving specimens reflect this.

What is the earliest surviving garment made from the cloth?

The nature of our climate and soils, together with the need to reuse garments and cloth in the past, means that few old examples of tartan survive. We have nothing that was created before the mid-18th century and only a number of examples associated with the Jacobites.

When was tartan's defining moment? When did it become noteworthy in historical terms?

If there's one date that is significant above all others it is 1822, the date of Sir Walter Scott's Royal Pageant and the tartan jamboree associated with George IV's visit to Scotland.

There appears to be a revival in the wearing of trews. Do you think this takes away from the Scottishness of tartan use?

No, why should it? Trews (*triubhas*) have been part of Highland dress since at least the 17th century, long before the development of the modern kilt.

When Sir Walter Scott was planning the Royal Pageant, many clan chieftains apparently had no idea what their tartan was. Or is this a myth?

In 1815 the Highland Society of London set about collecting 'traditional clan tartans' in order to preserve them. They wrote to the clan chiefs asking them to submit a specimen of their clan tartan. The trouble was that the idea that there had been such a thing as clan tartans was a recent invention.

The Society's correspondence reveals that most of the chiefs had no idea what their 'true clan' tartan was. The chief of MacPherson supplied a tartan that only a few years before had been a Wilsons' fancy pattern which they called No.43, Kidd or Caledonia. So many chiefs submitted a piece of government (Black Watch) tartan, probably because they'd served in the army, that the Society's officers had to restrict the number that they would accept.

The world is becoming a global village. Is it important for tartan to be celebrated and held in high esteem around the world?

For me, it's more important to preserve an understanding of the historical use and traditions of tartans for future generations. I was fortunate to have met and learned from some of the significant tartan researchers of the past – now there's just me. Where is the next generation and how do we collate and preserve our history? The work of the Scottish Tartans Authority is important in helping to preserve knowledge but there's always more to do.

What is the most obscure tartan that you know of?

Goodness, where to start? The Scottish Tartans Authority has over 9,000 tartans on its database; fewer than one hundred pre-date 1800, so my answer would have to be one of the early 18th-century cloths.

Undoubtedly the most obscure tartan, in terms of rarity and uniqueness, is that from the only known surviving coat of the Ancient Caledonian Society (ACS). The coat, which is in the collection of the Scottish Tartans Authority, dates to c1786 when the ACS was formed. The previously unknown tartan was almost certainly designed for the Society and is unusual in having a decorative silk motif woven into it. On each of the red squares there is a white rose and two buds representing King James VIII/III and the Princes Charles and Henry. The use of such obvious Jacobite iconography only thirty-three years after the last execution of a Jacobite leader is extraordinary and shows just how safe it had become to make such references without fear of reprisal. Tartan, with a secondary design such as the rose motif, would have been woven on an early Jacquard-type loom, probably outside of Scotland, possibly in Norwich which was famous for this type of weaving.

Do you have a favourite, little known story about the cloth you could share?

I wove the material for Prince William and Prince Harry's first kilts. The tartan was the Prince Charles Edward, an early variation of the Royal Stewart tartan, which is said to have been worn as ribbons on the wedding coat of Charles II.

Thirty-odd years later, I was privileged to work on a version of the Prince Charles Edward Stewart tartan that the Scottish Tartans Authority gifted to HRH Prince Charles, now King Charles; a tartan which he often wears when in Scotland.

A NOTE ON THE THREAD PALETTE

Yarn colours have all manner of intriguing names, but tartans have a more uniform range of colours for their variants. This consistency gives traditonal clan tartans their formality. Today new tones are combined to create more modern and fashion-relevant designs.

Each chapter opens with details of the colours of a particular tartan, stating the thread palette used to create the tartan. In these lists, Anc = ancient, and Rep = reproduction.

FAMILY

TARTAN
Murray of Atholl Weathered

Rep green
Rep black
Rep blue
Rep scarlet

SENSES OF IDENTITY

To strike a very personal note, it seems that the word 'family' today evokes something extraordinarily precious, but also something which can cause 90 per cent of your happiness or 90 per cent of your misery. But, nevertheless, lineage and belonging are, and always were, part of our most basic biology and fundamental sense of identity.

Thanks to our global community and intensely connective social networks, understanding where we've come from and either upholding our family's reputation or changing the direction of our stars is now more possible than ever.

CLANSHIP

My own upbringing was at the forefront of ground-breaking social change, by which I mean it was unconventional, in the traditional sense of the previous generation. Today it would be nothing out of the ordinary. As I was growing up my friends were my family, reflecting the old saying, 'You can choose your friends, but you can't choose your family.'

If we hark right back to the distant past, the people living and gathering in a district or an area would consider themselves a clan, and therefore fall under a group name, and what is family if not that? And, of course, some families developed reputations for warmongering, or for being English collaborators; they stood out for reasons of violent behaviour or political allegiances. Some things never change.

One of my favourite historical maps of Scotland is one which depicts the land according to the clans. I like the idea of a strong sense of belonging somewhere specific – and being able to see that mapped in clear visual form. Evidently, this is something in which I am not alone.

ALL ABOUT THE CLAN

The history of the clan system dates back to around the start of the fourth century BC, and although this isn't a history lecture, it's good to know that the Gaelic 'clan' means 'children' and the idea of clanship evolved from the times of the Druids. In England your name often comes from the type of job you undertook: Thatcher, Cook, Taylor, Smith and Millar are all examples of this. In Scotland, as communities were so isolated in many regions, it was more natural for you to take on the name of the area or the main family from that area.

For centuries the clan system was the hierarchical structure for the whole of Scotland. Each clan chief ruled his land and his people under the watchful rule of the King of Scotland. Clans might war with each other in disputes over land, but this system gave people a strong sense of shared identity and belonging. The official structure still resides today and is very different to the heraldic system in England and Wales. In Scotland the structure is regulated by the Court of the Lord Lyon, under the guise of coats of arms and Scottish heraldry. To have a coat of arms in Scotland is quite a serious undertaking, one that's policed by the Lord Lyon to ensure legitimacy and legality.

Scottish clans still have their chieftains, but their role is less warmongering and more sociable these days. Those clans without a chief are classed as 'armigerous clans'; they are not recognised as 'noble' communities and lack legal standing under Scots law. The noble clans often had an ancestral castle or great house, which acted as the hub for the councils of the region.

The two main concepts for clanship are very distinct. The first was of collective ancestry, or their 'dùthchas', which gave the right to settle in certain areas; the leading figures and the gentry of the clan would give protection and the clansmen would recognise this authority. The second was connected with the granting of charters by the crown. Known as 'oighreachd', this gave the chief or the laird authority over the land, making them responsible not only for the people but the land on which their people lived too.

Scots law shaped the structuring of the clans in Scotland from the Middle Ages onwards, ensuring succession of bloodlines. The heir to the chief was to be of direct bloodline, but often it would be given to someone more politically wise and so better suited for the role. It all got a little tangled in the 16th century with disputes over the legitimacy to rule a clan. To enable territory to remain strong and unified, the Law of Entail was introduced; this stopped lands being divided up among female heirs if no male heir was apparent.

A SHARED ANCESTRY

The main reason for taking a family name was lineal descent or bloodlines. You might also be adopted by a clan in a show of solidarity or to join together to fight. But in the main, clan membership was driven by the need for basic protection and sustenance. It was only really in the 16th century that the clan name became more commonly used as a surname. So, although you might be a Murray, you're not necessarily directly related to the clan chief by blood: it's more that you are 'of' the Murray clan.

Together with the fact that the meaning in Gaelic of 'children' can include those under the care of a family, this dispels that myth that all those with a Scottish surname are descended from one single ancestor.

And, to connect clanship with tartan, tartan became the cloth of a region and then the cloth of that region's most predominant family. The wealthiest, most powerful families could afford the most complicated weaves and the more diverse mix of colours in their cloth. This held true for both the highland and lowland areas of Scotland.

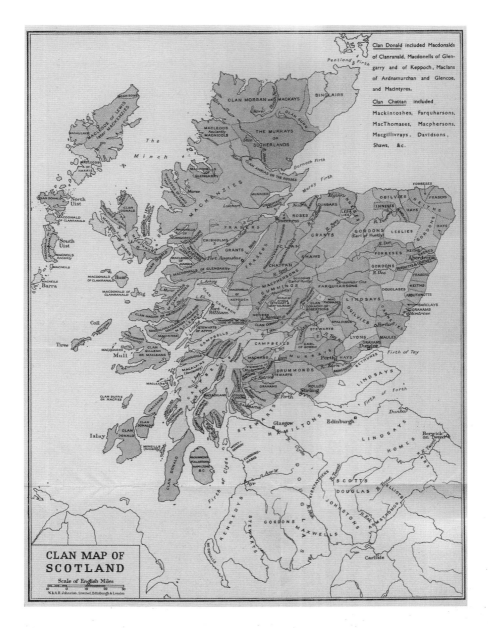

Clan Donald included Macdonalds of Clanranald, Macdonald of Glengarry and of Keppoch, Maclans of Ardnamurchan and Glencoe, and Macintyres.

Clan Chattan included Mackintoshes, Farquharsons, MacThomases, Macphersons, Macgillivrays, Davidsons, Shaws, &c.

CLAN MAP OF
SCOTLAND

Scale of English Miles

W. & A. K. Johnston, Limited, Edinburgh & London

CONTACT WITH ANCESTORS

The whole need, or want, that people have to find connections and meaning in their own lives via the people of their past (and then perhaps to brag about it) has generated a multimillion-pound industry. Those millions are not simply revenue from websites testing your DNA, but from all those spin-off ideas of heritage and belonging: from tartan to tours, from clan regalia to books and TV shows, from keyrings to castles. All there to feed a passion and thirst for knowledge.

The flipside to this is that some of Scotland's long-established families have a proud (or not quite so proud) lineage which can be traced directly back to an illustrious, impressive past. It's fascinating – and quite remarkable – to meet people who aren't making it up when they tell you their ancestors fought with Robert the Bruce, or which side some other ancestors fought for at the Battle of Culloden in 1746.

SUMMERTIME KILTS

And then there are the sometimes-painful experiences where these two passions for family collide with an intriguing combination of the joyous and the cringeworthy. For me, the main one I encounter on an almost weekly basis, particularly in the summer months, is from our transatlantic cousins

as they travel to Scotland to discover their Scottish ancestry. It's a complete delight to hear their enthusiasm for any tenuous links they might have to a Scottish heritage. Their willingness to wear tartan, to don the kilt, to embrace the culture and the romance of our fair nation is glorious to see.

There is always one visitor who goes one step further. This visitor has already done their research and approached a particular clan chieftain to ask his permission for themselves or their offspring to be allowed to wear the clan tartan in kilt or other form. It might seem a little fussy, but this is actually the correct thing to do. It's an act of protocol that shows a real respect, as well as good manners. There's a deference to what were once the 'ruling' classes of Scotland – which they repay by retaining their willingness to lead – and

to do this for the benefit of their clan and people. This instilled sense of responsibility to the land and its people has kept Scotland proud.

WOVEN ON HARRIS

One of my favourite stories of how the history and texture of cloth is woven into our lives encompasses both tartan and tweed; it's a tale that birthed an industry which now reaches the world over. Starting from an idea on a remote part of the Isle of Harris on the Outer Hebrides, this is the story of the beginning of the Harris Tweed industry. To be clear, it didn't just 'occur', nor has it always been there.

The cloth on Harris was a coarse yarn, with a loose weave, and it was initially woven by the island's crofters to be sold locally at market. It was made from local wool,

dyed using the colours taken from plants – including madder (indigo), slow-growing rock lichens (green), crotal (umber) and woad (brownish-yellow) – all using the island's diverse landscapes and woven on pedal looms: barely a luxury cloth back in 1846.

A DUNMORE STORY

It was in this year that Lady Dunmore, widow of the Earl of Dunmore, commissioned her family tartan – the Murray of Atholl – to be woven in tweed. The palette of muted blues and greens with a vivid red check was easily created by the island's resources, and it translated well from a distinctive pattern into more muted tones. When you are on Harris and Lewis you are starkly aware that what comes from the island really does come from the island!

Initially Lady Dunmore had asked for the

cloth to be woven for her estate workers, including the gamekeepers. It was perhaps a logical step to ask the local weavers to produce a uniform, but the gamekeepers needed to blend with the landscape, and perhaps the red check was more suited to fashion than to the functionality required on the island. The new cloth proved hugely successful on the social scene and, as more and more requests came from London and Edinburgh, she devoted much of her time to marketing the cloth and expanding its appeal. With her enthusiasm and energy, Harris Tweed quickly established itself as popular with merchants and tailors alike.

Thanks to it being in such demand as a darling of the social circles, it wasn't long before the trend for Harris Tweed filtered down to more and more parts of society until it became a genuine national sensation. The turn of the century saw the industry in full swing and investment was put into machinery to meet the ever-growing demand.

Then, in 1906 a standardisation of quality was required, which held that the cloth would need to be inspected and stamped as meeting the criteria for authenticity. This saw the setting up of the Harris Tweed Association and the introduction of the Dunmore Orb and Maltese cross as the certification mark; the first stamp as we know it today appeared in 1910.

gamekeepers' plus-fours and jackets. The colours were echoing the land, but the cloth was certainly coarse and heavy.

Do you know the name of the person commissioned to weave it? Or was it one of the mills who offered the service?
There's no definite existence of the name of the weaver or crofter I'm afraid; I suppose much of the commissioning was verbal and not written at that time. Although there is a story that Lady Catherine approached two lady weavers in the village of Strond. Locally known as the Paisley Sisters, they were renowned for their higher-quality finish: having been trained on the mainland, their technique was more refined.

Q&A: LADY DUNMORE

Through the tangle of my own social connections – and the generosity of Lady Dunmore herself – I was lucky enough to gain an introduction to the current Lady Dunmore. Even more luckily, she agreed to be quizzed about all this amazing Isle of Harris history and the secrets it can tell us about both tartan and tweed.

Vixy Rae: What was the tartan which was woven into the tweed? Murray or Murray of Atholl?
Lady Dunmore: Murray of Atholl, but also Murray of Tullibardine, which is a slightly brighter and more complex weave.

What were the first garments which were commissioned from the cloth?
The initial garments were the estate

Family heirlooms? Do any survive of that first cloth?
I am only aware of two lengths of the original fabric. These are the curtains made for Amhuinnsuidhe Castle in the Murray of Tullibardine tartan. They certainly drape well and keep out the draughts.

What is your favourite tartan piece in your wardrobe?
My absolute favourite tartan garment is the silk tartan dress I commissioned for my daughter's wedding. It is vibrant and elegant, lovingly hand-crafted which makes it a pleasure to wear.

If you were to commission a pattern to be woven from Harris Tweed, what would it be?

There are so many beautiful patterns which translate through different uses of colour, it's not a simple question to answer. Depth and texture are what attract me to a pattern when it comes to tweed. The classics are always a favourite and are never wrong.

Do you have many pieces of Harris Tweed in your wardrobe?

I do own many pieces constructed from Harris Tweed; there is something functional and beautiful about the cloth. My favourites are simple skirts and jackets, timeless and wearable.

At social events do you find it important to wear tartan?

I do like to wear tartan for formal occasions, but only when it is correct or if there is a Scottish theme.

And which do you prefer – tweed or tartan?

Both, naturally.

Can you tell me more about Lady Catherine? For a woman at that time it must have been quite something to push a new cloth from the Outer Hebrides?

Lady Dunmore (Catherine) became the link between the weavers and the market for their tweed and advised them on colour palette and design.

In 1841, Lady Catherine was appointed as the Lady of the Bedchamber to Queen Victoria. This was an official position of great privilege, being a personal attendant to the queen. Sadly, Lady Catherine resigned upon the death of her husband four years later. At this point she inherited the 150,000 acres of Dunmore Estate along with Amhuinnsuidhe Castle on the Isle of Harris.

She made many improvements to the estate village, including the building of a new school and the laying of a village green. However, it was during the Highland Potato Famine of 1846 that Lady Catherine became involved in the promotion and economic development of Harris Tweed as a product. Resources on the Isle of Harris are scarce, which is something you really notice when you are there. The weaving industry created a good sustainable product with potential for growth, which had certain unique qualities that set it apart from other tweeds.

Lady Catherine was clever in recognising the fabric's potential, which, although less refined, held a wonderful richness to its colour depth and a rugged texture. The biggest hurdles to jump were the irregularities, particularly in the dyeing, spinning and weaving. The cloth had much competition from machine-made cloths, as nearly all parts of the Harris Tweed process at this point were done purely by hand – leading to those inconsistencies in weight, texture and colour.

Modern techniques needed to be introduced; Lady Catherine organised and financed training sessions in Alloa to ensure skills and refinements in production were passed to the Islands. She was very driven, as she could see the potential for growth. She even allowed the islanders to use her orb as the cloth's symbol.

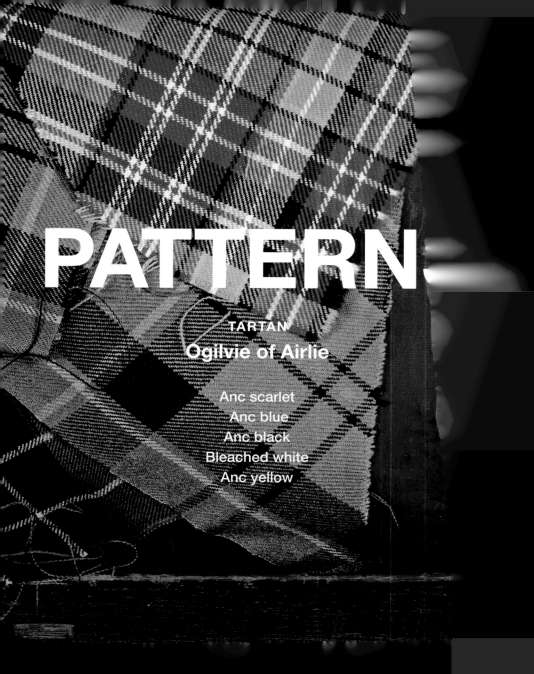

PATTERN

TARTAN

Ogilvie of Airlie

Anc scarlet
Anc blue
Anc black
Bleached white
Anc yellow

A number of features specifically denote a tartan, but the colour and the pattern remain the most important of these. Tartan is a woven fabric, which means the strands or threads are interlaced into each other to create the cloth.

WARP, WOOF AND TWILL

The woven cloth is made up of the 'warp' and the 'weft' (or, delightfully, 'woof' depending where you live). The warp is the longest thread which runs the length of the cloth, and the weft is the thread which goes across the width of the cloth.

When it comes to weaving there are hundreds of books that will help turn you into an expert, but here are the basics. The earliest and simplest weave is called 'plain' weave. Plain weave is one strand over and one strand under; this gives a flat and simple weave, the form of which dates back from the very earliest days of weaving.

Tartan is made up from what is called a 'twill' weave; this is the next level on from the straightforwardness of the plain weave. In its simplest form, twill is two strands under and two strands over. This gives a distinctive diagonal line across the cloth. This line is known as the 'wale' and it becomes more obvious and pronounced when the yarn becomes thicker.

The rationale of this twill weave is that it is very stable, which means it holds the pattern well. The tension of the yarn and tightness of the weave give it durability; they offer, to a certain degree, a level of stain and crease resistance.

There are varying complexities that work together to achieve a tartan pattern. Some of the simplest tartans barely look like tartan as we might think of it today. The one adopted by Sir Walter Scott for the Great Pageant of August 1822 resembled a tweed shepherd's check, and likewise the Rob Roy tartan only uses two colours to achieve its bold, dramatic effect. The only reason these two examples are not classed as tweed is that the yarn is brighter and more refined, creating a clearer and more distinctive pattern.

The earliest examples of the cloth we know as tartan are often perceived as tweed; so, even from the days of the Celts and the Druids, there is a blurring of ideas and boundaries. However, as weaving has developed, looms have become increasingly more complex; this means they are able to produce more consistent and longer lengths of cloth.

THE STORY OF THE LOOM

If we look back into history, looms started their lives as vertical, with the longest thread, the warp being tensioned by weight and gravity. Weaving was a very labour-intensive process and individuals from the local community would often bring the weaver yarn or fleece to make up and to be paid in kind.

Because the weft thread needed to be passed across through the warp by hand, the width of cloth remained the same for many centuries. The development of the 'flying shuttle' in 1733 made the job significantly easier – while the master weaver checked the warp, the apprentice would be in charge of throwing the weft thread through the loom.

The technology of weaving is a fascinating, intricate subject, but I am trying to avoid too much technical detail! Suffice to say, as time passed people made those inevitable refinements to looms and spinning which made life a lot easier and also gave a better finish to the cloth. If the fleece could be drawn out further while spinning, then the resulting yarn would be finer. Likewise, if the tensioning of the yarn on the loom was maintained by a mechanism rather than a person, the weave would be more consistent and more tightly formed. The dawn of the Industrial Revolution was key to making these refinements, creating fabrics of better quality and consistency. It opened up opportunity for large-scale production, for wider looms creating cloth

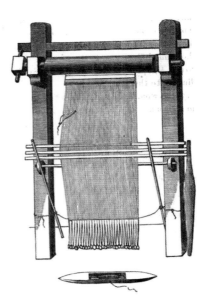

more stable and more durable, but also luxury cloth could now be produced under the same process, changing the way we dress for ever.

A SIGNIFICANT SWITCH

In the early 19th century the vertical loom was replaced with the horizontal loom. At the same time, the control of the warp was given over to foot rather than hand, which made it easier for one person alone to manage a loom. This meant a weaver could operate the warp threads with a treadle, leaving his hands free to throw the shuttle. I say 'his' as this was a very physical job which required an amount of mechanical expertise: the majority of weavers were men.

The female aspect was in the finer aspects of cloth making and perhaps the more mundane ones too; most notably washing, scouring, carding and spinning . . . all the processes which created the raw material.

The Industrial Revolution saw the automation of the looms and changes to cloth width. For centuries, cloth had been 'single width' at around 70cm to 74cm. Now that the shuttle was passed by mechanics rather than by hand, this width could be doubled to 140cm to 154cm. As their product – woven cloth – became more refined and cheaper to produce by machine, much of the community of weaving, like so many others, fell away during the years following the Industrial Revolution.

THE MUSIC OF WEAVING

Today we call single-width cloth 'hand loomed'. If you visit a mill, they will probably have a single-width loom or a Hattersley loom, which can be used to make sample lengths or short runs of cloth. Stay a while and listen if you can. There is something deeply comforting and melodic about the noise from a Hattersley loom, which speaks of its secret life. I hear the steady pace and clatter of the pedals and the shuttles as a mechanical symphony. You can imagine the weavers and their apprentices singing along to the pace of the loom to while away their hours. The repetitive rhythm of the loom gave pace to those undertaking the preparation

of the fleece too, giving a musical flow to their work.

It's a complex, mathematical process to set up a loom. Of course, it's utterly logical, but for me there's magic in it too. These days the warp boom is the part which takes time and precision to set up; that's followed by the cones of yarn for the weft shuttles. But what about the pattern?

SETTING THE PATTERN

Each tartan has a 'sett', and this relates to the position and number of threads required to create a particular pattern.

In the main each tartan is either 'symmetrical' or 'asymmetrical'. I have found, as a tailor, that the asymmetrical ones are a nightmare to work with. Luckily, symmetrical ones are a lot more common. A sett is usually created to fit onto the width of the cloth, so each sett has a 'pivot' point where the pattern is repeated in reverse after a certain point. This is getting technical again, but I will do my best to explain.

Let's start with the simpler tartans. MacGregor – more commonly known as the Rob Roy – has only two colours: black and red. The warp and weft are set up in the same manner as each other. Eight strands of red and eight strands of black then pivot and repeat on the weft. This then gives an alternate 16 strands of black and red on the warp.

As families grew and combined, other colours were sometimes added to denote the generational changes. An example of

this might be the introduction of a new colour and line to jump from Rob Roy tartan to Wallace tartan. Whereby two strands of black and two strands of golden yellow are introduced and used as the new pivot points.

BLK 2, RED 16, BLK 16, YLW 2.

The predominant colour here – the golden yellow – would be considered the centre of the sett.

This way of recording the thread count seems consistent through the ages as the patterns of tartan were changed and then handed down. But there is a myth that we need to tackle next – a myth which revolves around something called a 'pattern stick'.

" The enormous
complexity of the
pattern makes it
impossible to say
whether accuracy
of design has been
maintained over the
years.

THE MYTH OF THE PATTERN STICK

It was noted in the 17th century that weavers would keep careful records of the exact numbers of strands in a pattern by wrapping the yarn around a piece of wood and numbering the strands. However, there are no surviving pattern sticks prior to the 1746 Act of Proscription of tartan, and any record of this method of recording seems to exist merely in writing rather than in physical form. My theory is that this myth grew from the sticks bearing the original dressing from a dismantled loom being mistaken for something more complex. Here we have another example of tartan's romantic tendencies, its propensity to turn the mundane into something other than what it is.

TARTAN ON RECORD

The first significant attempt to record tartan patterns was an 1831 book titled *The Scottish Gael.* This considerable work by James Logan consists of 54 patterns but seems to be more of a 'fashion book' than a technical guide, as many experts have since found inaccuracies in both sett and colour, making it perhaps history's first art/ coffee-table book on tartan.

The most reliable archive of the records of tartan seems to be that from the Main and Predominant Mill, created in the late 17th century by William Wilson of Bannockburn. Sadly, this mill is no longer in operation, but its legend and legacy live on; it will always be an integral part of the history of tartan.

The synchronicity of the Industrial Revolution and subsequent creation of power looms and textile mills with Sir Walter Scott's landmark idea to hold a pageant for George VI in 1822 has always seemed extraordinary to me. What a coincidence . . . But with supplies more readily available and a better consistency to the cloth it is perhaps no wonder that tartan became more in vogue from this period onwards.

TARTAN EN VOGUE

The two bestselling tartans in the history of Wilson's of Bannockburn were those sold directly after the 1822 pageant. They were the King George IV and the Sir Walter Scott. What I'd like to know is – did Sir Walter receive royalties for the cloth he designed?

LOOMS OF BANNOCKBURN

The firm of William Wilson & Sons quickly became the go-to company for anything to do with tartan and patterns. They ensured they had the backing of tartan experts, and this in turn enabled them to have their patterns endorsed. Thus, theirs were recognised as the truly authentic patterns, and they used these to prepare the definitive pattern book of the age. This was then sent to London, to the Highland Society of London for certification. Their pattern book held 240 tartans,130 of which were named, and the rest were simply numbered awaiting clan and family association.

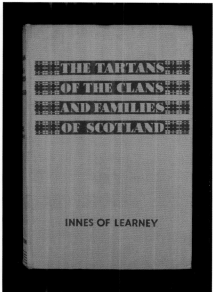

INTO THE 21ST CENTURY

Tartan's status and popularity has enjoyed a natural progression from this point onwards with the raising of the Highland regiments after the Jacobite Rising to police the wild areas of Scotland and then again when Queen Victoria came to the throne. Her love for the cloth – she was very much what we might now call a royal brand ambassador for tartan – meant it again became the height of fashion not just for clothing but also for interiors and soft furnishings.

It was inevitable that the setts would become more complex and the colours would follow the trends of the time, from the Antonine tartan of two colours to the Ogilvie of Airlie tartan with its ridiculously complex sett and over 180 colour changes.

Today, in the 21st century, Lochcarron of Scotland lead the way in the production of tartan, supplying the cloth on an international scale to families, companies and designers alike. I was fortunate enough to be given a tour around their mill. With its state-of-the-art design and computerised weaving, tartan production has certainly checked into the modern age. What follows is what I learned on my Lochcarron visit.

YARN DYEING: THE PROCESS BEGINS

Yarns are wound onto cones or springs and are then dyed in dye vats. There are 'recipe cards' for each colour that is dyed and a reference is kept of each batch dyed.

The dye powder is mixed with water and the yarn is dyed in a sealed vat where the water/dye is circulated. The temperature is around 100 degrees and the time in the dye vat can be up to two hours; darker shades usually take the longest. Next the liquid is drained off and the wet cones of yarn are spun to remove more of the liquid. Drying is done on racks in ovens and takes around eight hours.

THE SECRETS OF PATTERNS AND WARPING

Each tartan has its own unique pattern and colours. These are recorded on the design ticket and the first process in creating fabric is preparing the warp.

This set of vertical threads make up each block of the pattern right across the width of the fabric 'from selvedge to selvedge'. The yarns are loaded on to the 'warp bank' to create one full repeat of the pattern sequence and each thread is drawn off the warp bank in the order of the pattern.

Each pattern sequence of threads is then wound around a large drum until it reaches the full length needed. This is tied off and the next block of the pattern is done in the same way for the same length until eventually all the pattern repeats that create the full width and length of the warp are completed. This is called the warp and, once completed, it is wound from the large drum onto a smaller beam ready to go forward for weaving.

WARP, WEFT AND WEAVING

It's the process of weaving that creates fabric. Each fabric has its own specifications in terms of the width, weight, density of threads and the type of weaving construction. Most tartans are constructed in a weave known as 2/2 twill where two warp threads lift over two weft threads in a sequence which gives the appearance of a series of diagonal lines running throughout the fabric.

The beam with the warp is lifted into the back of the loom and each warp thread is pulled through a series of 'heddles' (metal wires with a hole for the yarn), which are hung on shafts and then pulled through a reed. The shafts lift up and down in the loom and the weft thread is inserted across the width of the warp between the warp threads, some of which are lifted up on some shafts or remain lowered on others (this is called the 'shed'). The reed keeps the warp threads running parallel to each other right across the full width in the loom.

The weft threads are inserted in the pattern sequence across the warp, and between each thread being inserted there is a mechanism which moves the reed forward to push the weft together so the cloth becomes more compacted.

So, the warp is constantly moving forward off the beam at the back of the loom and when the weft is inserted the fabric is pushed forward and wound onto a beam at the front of the loom.

PRESENT AND CORRECT

All fabrics are inspected at the start of the weaving process to make sure the pattern and construction is correct. Once the pieces – the lengths of fabric – are woven they are inspected by 'darners', whose role it is to check the cloth by touch and sight for any knots or faults. These are then mended by the darners before the fabrics go forward to the cloth-finishing stage.

AND TO FINISH

Finishing is a series of processes involving washing and drying the fabrics to create cloth ready for subsequent uses such as garment making.

Washing is done at a variety of temperatures for different lengths of time and with differing amounts of 'agitation' during the process, which varies depending upon the cloth finish that's required.

Once washed, an initial drying process is completed in a machine called a 'tenter' where the cloth is stretched out under tension and the selvedges are held on a series of metal prongs known as 'tenter hooks'. This brilliantly obscure part of a complex process is where the saying 'on tenter hooks' comes from. Who knew!

Additional aspects of the finishing process can include milling, brushing, cropping and 'decatising' – the latter is also known as crabbing, blowing or decating. All of which are selected depending upon the cloth finish required.

Q&A: DAWN ROBSON-BELL
Managing director, Lochcarron of Scotland

Vixy Rae: What was the first tartan garment you can remember wearing as a child? And did you like it?

Dawn Robson-Bell: I've a black-and-white photo of me and the family dog when I must have been maybe seven. Usually I'd be in scruffy jeans and a T-shirt, but we must have been going somewhere and my mam has managed to get me into a skirt! Actually, I'm sure it was a whole ensemble: a Royal Stewart pleated skirt with braces and a white blouse, all joined together and pulled on! It must have been my 'good outfit' and I do remember liking it otherwise Mam would never have gotten me into it. However, my hair is still a scruffy straggly mess so she must have decided that battle wasn't worth fighting!

How long have you been working with fabric, and at Lochcarron?

I graduated from Heriot-Watt in 1987 with an honours degree in textile design. I was lucky enough to work with two textile companies during my time at college, which really helped my understanding of woven textile design and manufacturing. I joined Lochcarron in 1988 on a temporary basis to help out in production. Basically I never left! My subsequent roles gave me wide and varied experiences, leading to my current position as MD. I'm not content just to work with textiles; I also enjoy patchwork and quilting and am lucky to be able to use scraps and off-cuts from the mill in lots of projects.

What has been the biggest change in your time with the company?

I can't pinpoint one thing but am aware that we've gone through lots of changes, from staff to premises to owners. However, we have a good core team of experienced staff and are more focused than ever on strengthening the team, bringing in new skills, starting apprenticeships and investing in machinery and systems that will ensure we have a long future ahead of us.

How many tartans do you hold in stock?

From our collections we can offer tartan in well over two thousand different options, from fabrics, to scarves, blankets to skirts, ties, caps and much more.

What's the most unusual tartan you have produced? And what were its colours?

Wow! There have been lots of projects over the years that are memorable for different reasons. I guess a giant-size kilt in a very green tartan was pretty memorable: we made it for Shrek for the London film première.

After Scotland and America, which is your next biggest global market?

It has to be Japan. The Japanese love tartan, not only the colours and patterns, but tartan's place in Scottish history and the sense of identity it portrays.

Which gets your vote – trews or kilts?

I like to think they both have their place. The great thing is having the two options gives people choices and hopefully lots will choose both!

How many tartan garments do you have in your own wardrobe?

Lots and lots of scarves, a few bags, but very few actual garments.

What is your favourite tartan? And why?

My favourites tend to be bold tartans. The Dress Macleod and Wallace or MacQueen are all fairly simple and real statement tartans with a sense of timelessness while also feeling very contemporary.

With all the romance surrounding tartan, what is your favourite tale of the cloth?

What really amazes me is just how many people worldwide recognise tartan and in particular specific tartans; for example, Black Watch and Royal Stewart. I really can't think of any other fabric patterns that would be so well known!

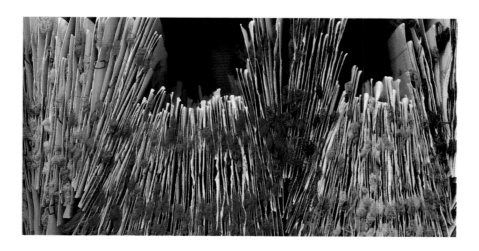

LOCAL

TARTAN
Fraser

Anc scarlet
Anc blue
Anc green

A HANDS-ON APPROACH

If I wanted a soapbox to stand on and preach, this chapter would be it. From an early age I was taught that the nurturing and possession of practical skills gave you the useful ability to be creative and productive. This ethos is one that's led me to be a great advocate of keeping much of the creative process as local as possible.

My schooling was delivered through the Steiner philosophy of education, and so my practical side was fostered; I was inspired to want to create. From cooking to needlework, woodcraft to horticulture, I learned the value of putting in genuine effort, time and patience. However, it's not difficult to see that these qualities are disappearing from the world at large at a rapid rate, lost in a blur of speed, profit and convenience.

The seemingly insatiable need for instant gratification, whether online or in 'real life', is offset by the notion of sustainability, which is becoming a buzz word of our times. We are told – castigated, even – to reduce, reuse and recycle. But no matter how much we talk about it, and how often we get on our moral high horses, unless we actually take positive action now, we will leave so many issues for our children to sort out that we will become, and rightfully so, the 'blamed' generation.

Of course, it's hardly unprecedented for each generation to blame the one before for the shortcomings of the current age, but the fact is we must figure out what we can do to ensure that craft and skill are taught and enthused about, otherwise we will come to exist in a world of innovators and designers, but no one will have the skills to realise any of the glorious things we conceptualise.

PROVENANCE

So, when I titled this chapter 'local' I really meant 'keeping it local', and this ethos goes for tartan as much as anything else of Scottish provenance. In my working life I have designed and created streetwear, and collections of ladies' tailoring, but no matter what the tailoring there's always that niggling thought that asks, 'Why aren't we making these things here?'

There was a significant decline in how Britain and indeed Scotland produced fabric and garments in the early 1990s. This bore witness to the need to be competitive on price and to produce the quantities required to meet demand. Seems we wanted everything now, and we wanted it cheap. Production slowly left these shores and headed east.

Larger companies were leaving the UK to produce in Europe and then further afield to Turkey, which acted as the gateway to the east, the next stop before India and finally China. The further east the lower the price, but the higher the quantity, which suited multinational garment companies down to the ground. There was the issue of quality, but when things are cheap perhaps people's expectations are lowered. In the worlds of fashion and textiles – which are two of the highest polluting industries – there's a need for reinvention every season, a monster which demands to be fed via the consumer, who signs up to this via the promise of glamorous brand marketing. After the greed of the 1980s, the ensuing austerity was replaced by a new era of consumerism.

THE PRODUCTION OF TARTAN

When it comes to tartan, the myth and the 'propaganda' in which the whole history of the cloth is wrapped, I believe the one thing that has 'kept it real' is the fact of tartan's production in Scotland using traditional skills handed down from generation to generation. Of course, there is the inevitable point where evolution beyond a cottage industry is necessary to supply a growing demand; even so, a genuine credibility and authenticity is conferred if tartan is produced and designed here in Scotland.

As much as I have noted an American tendency to rediscover a Scottish lineage, perhaps we could simply supply what is longed for and complete their story. Today, if you walk along Edinburgh's Royal Mile, stretching from the castle to Holyrood Palace, there's a melancholy mix of shops aimed at the visitor market. In their offer, some have taken notions from Scottish popular culture and exploited them. From tartan towels to Harry Potter T-shirts, the amount of merchandise produced outwith Scotland and the UK is disturbing.

The Scottish souvenir market can be traced to Victorian times and Tartanware. There's still plenty of it about – wooden boxes, pin cushions and trinkets created locally and decorated with a tartan pattern, mostly Royal Stewart. But these days, souvenir tartan has lost its soul – and its provenance. There are tartan kilts made from cloth woven in India and manufactured in Bangladesh, and tweed jackets made from 'Shetland' tweed, woven and manufactured in Portugal.

I can't help but question this – is it right that the essence of Scottishness is an image, a mere symbol? The insistence that quality comes second to profit margins seems like a consumer hangover from which the more discerning traveller is slowly awakening. I'm hopeful that this new breed of visitor is creating a different kind of demand that needs to be met.

AN AUTHENTIC HOME

The baby boom generation – and much younger millennials too – are reaching the stage where they are deeply tired of mass-produced soulless product for product's sake. They are looking for that which is authentic, of a tangible quality and unique. They recognise that these attributes come at a price, not because the makers are greedy, but simply because the costs of production are significantly higher. This is as true for a pair of tartan trews as it is a tartan-lined handbag.

Even so, tartan *is* tartan – it's a pattern, a colour palette and a weave – and perhaps questioning its 'authenticity' is pointless; surely it can be created in Scotland, in India or anywhere at all? Whether we grant it a symbolic significance or whether we appreciate its peerless design, the reality is Scotland didn't create checked cloth. Tartan-like fabric, which pre-dates the Falkirk 'tartan', has been found on glacial mummies in the Far East, so either the Scots travelled a lot and got into trouble, or

a global consciousness and progression led weavers on from plain to stripe to check.

Scotland did, however, embrace the fabric, giving it a name, a home, a purpose and a history. This identity is now internationally recognised as key to this small nation of pride, passion and creativity . . . of union and rebellion, all wrapped in a tartan philibeg.

THE CRAFT OF SLOWING DOWN

My own journey from streetwear to tailoring made me appreciate just how vital education and skills are. When I first took over Stewart Christie & Co., it was clear that, given the traditional professionalism and quality of its garments, this remarkable heritage would run into difficulties if our skills weren't passed on, nurtured and enhanced by a younger generation. I feel the responsibility keenly: this is something I couldn't allow to slowly disappear. Without education and shared learning, all our skills will fade away.

These thoughts were in my mind when I attended an end-of-year award ceremony at Dumfries House, in Ayrshire. It's a 'modern model estate', one where the outbuildings have been transformed into education centres to teach students practical skill-based courses. All skills taught benefit the estate, but the sense is of something real that people can share; you can feel their sense of pride and commitment through the work.

An inspirational speech by His Royal Highness the Duke of Rothesay at this ceremony sparked a depth of emotion in me. Talking about the importance of nurturing hand crafts, he used the phrase 'a black hole of traditional crafts', which sums up perfectly how we are being helplessly drawn into a future with a void of skills, unless we do something about it – and now.

THE TAILORING OF SKILLS

With tartan such a landmark aspect of Scottish dress and identity, I am pleased to say there are now more opportunities to learn kilt-making in Scotland than ever before; from intensive full-time courses to 'taster workshops' to a more relaxed series of evening classes, the intricacies and joys of making a traditional kilt are accessible to all.

However, hand-sewing is only part of the story. The simple fact is you wouldn't just wear a kilt . . . unless you're a kilted yoga boy! Rather, it's the tailoring side of Highland wear which seems to be hurtling towards the precipice. The styling and fit of Highland jackets and doublets are very unique and follow specific (yet flexible) rules to do with occasion and proportion. These garments are something very few bespoke London tailors would choose to construct. I wonder sometimes if these skills are seen as a 'dark art' by our professional peers in England?

There is a way forward, and it's one I've been pushing for since I first took control of Stewart Christie. In conjunction with Edinburgh College and Clydebank, we've worked to address the need for a Scottish Vocational Qualification in Bespoke Tailoring. The talent pool of Savile Row has long been nurtured by a college and foundation course, along with a pledge to take on a certain number of apprentices. Thus, the tailoring craft maintains a necessary balance between those retiring and those entering into the trade, while enabling diversity to flourish. In Scotland, this new SVQ has begun to safeguard tailoring's future as a forward-thinking, deeply skilful and wide-ranging occupation.

I always find it refreshing how many like-minded folk there are who want to drive ideas and notions forward. It's a truism that the connectivity of social media makes it far easier to bring people and ideas together, but it's how we act on them and make them into something credible and real that matters. Tailoring must seek to create that which is attractive to younger generations, but the craft of tailoring in itself won't cut it. We also need on side those who are knowledgeable, dedicated and in tune enough to motivate a youth culture, those used to admiring, seeing, purchasing, modifying all at the instant tap of a screen. These are the ones we need to understand that not everything in life is instant. The fact is that learning a skill takes time, patience and instruction, but we as the teachers are the ones responsible for generating enthusiasm.

A WORLD OF CONVENIENCE

The world seems to have spun itself into a bit of a hurry, and I would like to slow it down, to be part of an education on simple truths. I often think of one of my favourite quotes from a customer, who told me, 'When I was a student, I was too poor to buy cheap clothes.' Which at first makes no sense until you understand he was referring to a tailored garment. Quality cloth and quality stitching create garments that will last much longer – holding their shape, texture and form – which can be altered, fitted and adjusted over time. Even when they are well worn and a little scuffed at the edges, they retain their character and don't take on the tired look of cheaper clothes. The rows of pre-loved kilts or soft piles of gentle cashmere at Scotland's vintage stores are testament to this. No one can deny the cost of tailored clothes, but it's worth matching it with the French philosophy of garment purchase: 'To find the actual cost of a garment, divide its price by the number of times you wear – and enjoy – it.' It's an ethos which promotes a realistic sustainability and reflects a time before the world discovered synthetic fibres and sportswear.

These ideas aren't a battle cry that seeks to stand in the way of progress; quite the opposite. I want the world of what we wear, of how we dress to be one of potential and pride, for there to be recognition for products which

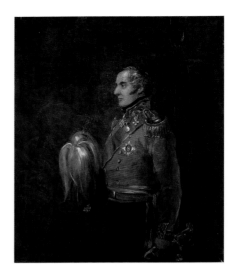

are completely homespun and sewn. I recognise a need for all levels of price point, but my heart sings at the thought of 'Keep it authentic. Keep it local.' And I know I'm not the only one who thinks this, a fact which tells me there is a bright future lurking behind the clouds of uncertainty.

That last sentence was beginning to sound a wee bit like a political speech . . . so I'll get down from my soapbox for now and allow you time to digest my manifesto! All I would ask is for you to 'vote' accordingly. The next time you purchase something – made of tartan or otherwise – which professes to be Scottish, delve deeper and ask yourself is it really 'Made in Scotland'?

Q&A: JOHN MCLEISH
Chairman of the Scottish
Tartans Authority

Vixy Rae: The Highland Society of London cataloged tartans back in the 19th century. Is the Scottish Tartans Authority a modern-day version of this?

John McLeish: I consider myself very fortunate to be a member of the Highland Society of London, which was instituted in 1778. It exists to promote and support the traditions of the Highlands of Scotland.

By contrast, the Scottish Tartans Authority was constituted as a Registered Charity in 1995 and is the successor organisation to the former Scottish Tartans Society. In broad terms, the Authority's purpose is to protect, preserve, conserve, promote and explain the culture, traditions and uses of Scottish tartans and Highland dress. We maintain a database of over 9,000 tartans and the core of this database was used to establish the Scottish Register of Tartans, a function of National Records of Scotland, in 2009. The Authority fields hundreds of enquiries about tartan and Highland dress each year and we work in partnership with a range of individuals as well as private and public organisations to achieve our charitable purposes.

What is your role within the Scottish Tartans Authority?

I joined the Authority as a member in 2010, became a trustee in 2011 and was elected Chair in 2012. I am one of a group of trustees who care passionately about tartan and its cultural significance to Scotland. I chair the board and have always sought to bring a commercial focus which, for a small charity with scarce resources, is absolutely vital. Having worked across a range of industry sectors including banking, passenger transport and oil services, I believe the common currency for success is people. My role is about bringing people together, whether it be from a culture and heritage background or from a broad tartan industry base, all for a common cause and with the best interests of tartan at the forefront of our minds.

What is your earliest memory of tartan?

I'm not sure that I have one single memory, but I do remember watching a pipe band parade while growing up in Perth and asking my mum if I could have a kilt. I was five years old. My first kilt was made from Fraser tartan in ancient red colours (my maternal grandmother was a Fraser), and I have never looked back.

The Scottish Tartans Authority collection must have some impressive pieces. For you, which is the most important historically?

Many people like to think of the history of tartan and Highland dress in terms of 'revolution'. In fact, it is much more about evolution and, so, different items within our collection mean different things to different people. Perhaps the Victorian era did more than any other to cement the image of the 'noble' Highlander and Queen Victoria was absolutely clear about this when she wrote in 1865, 'I think the Highlanders are the finest race in the world.'

The queen went further than this when she commissioned *Highlanders of Scotland*, published in 1870, which consisted of two leather-bound volumes of watercolour portraits by Kenneth Macleay RSA. There are thirty-one portraits in all, detailing fifty-seven individual Highlanders, each depicted with the utmost accuracy in terms of tartan and Highland dress. We are very lucky to own an original set of these volumes.

Do you have a favourite piece in the Scottish Tartans Authority's collection?

An elaborate sporran, dating from 1815, that forms part of a Highland outfit made for the Duke of Sussex, brother of George IV and uncle to Queen Victoria.

Why is this sporran so meaningful to you?

Of all the elements that make up Highland dress, the sporran is the least well documented and yet, over the years, has become the most individual and visible Highland dress 'accessory'. In recent years, the Scottish Tartans Authority has worked hard to support Scottish sporran makers and, when you see a sporran like the one described above, it's clear that the art of

quality sporran making requires high levels of skill, precision and craftsmanship. It is good to see a growing number of orders for bespoke sporrans – how better to express a person's individuality?

There seems to be more 'handed down' history about tartan than actual fact. Does this give the cloth more appeal and allure?

I'm absolutely clear that the story of tartan is one of 'feelings' versus 'fabric'. Without the feelings that tartan evokes, the fabric itself lacks provenance and gravitas – there would be no tartan industry without these feelings, and the telling of stories and the passing on of information from generation to generation is really what history is about. Legend, myth, historical events, fashion, family, celebration . . . I could go on about many more elements that make up the story of tartan and all of these most certainly do add to the appeal and allure of our iconic national cloth.

The Scottish Tartans Authority sometimes takes on commissions. Do any of these stand out in your memory?

The Scottish Tartans Authority doesn't, generally, take on commissions for the design of tartan. The reason for this is very simple: we want to support our members rather than compete with them. We are very fortunate and honoured to have a supportive Patron in HRH Prince Charles, now King Charles, and last year, in celebration of His Royal Highness's 70th birthday, we designed a tartan for The Prince's Foundation, the sett based on that of Old Stewart as first recorded in the 1819 Key Pattern book of William Wilson & Son of Bannockburn. This was a most enjoyable project and it is very fitting that a Stewart (David) was the first Duke of Rothesay between 1398 and 1402.

There is a resurgence of artisan weaving occurring throughout Scotland. Do you think it is important for the cloth to be woven in Scotland, to keep it truly authentic?

I would like more tartan to be woven in Scotland but, more importantly, I believe it would be helpful for tartan cloth to be more easily identified in terms of its source. Tartan is manufactured in many countries and in many fabrics – this is not something we can or should strive to change. What we should do, however, is support and encourage those indigenous weavers who work extremely hard to produce a high-quality fabric for the enjoyment of a diverse customer base across the world.

What does the future hold for the Scottish Tartans Authority?

The future is bright but, then again, it would be as the future is tartan! The trustees will continue in our quest to promote, protect and preserve tartan and Highland dress and we very much hope to fulfil our ambition to create a National Tartan Centre that will showcase and promote tartan, and its important Highland heritage as well as its iconic status as the defining symbol of a nation. Watch this space!

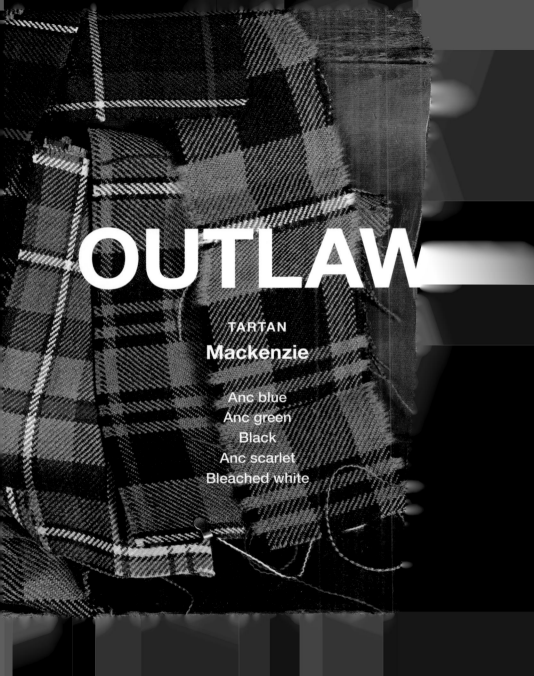

OUTLAW

TARTAN
Mackenzie

Anc blue
Anc green
Black
Anc scarlet
Bleached white

ABOLITION AND PROSCRIPTION OF HIGHLAND DRESS 19 GEORGE II CHAPTER 39, SEC. 17, 1746

That from and after the first day of August, One thousand, seven hundred and forty-six, no man or boy within that part of Britain called Scotland, other than such as shall be employed as Officers and Soldiers in His Majesty's Forces, shall, on any pretext whatever, wear or put on the clothes commonly called Highland clothes (that is to say) the Plaid, Philabeg, or little Kilt, Trowse, Shoulder-belts, or any part whatever of what peculiarly belongs to the Highland Garb; and that no tartan or party-coloured plaid of stuff shall be used for Great Coats or upper coats, and if any such person shall presume after the said first day of August, to wear or put on the aforesaid garment or any part of them, every such person so offending . . . For the first offence, shall be liable to be imprisoned for 6 months, and on the second offence, to be transported to any of His Majesty's plantations beyond the seas, there to remain for the space of seven years.

THE CLOTHES COMMONLY CALLED

This above edict was the wording by which the English crown attempted to stamp out any future sparks of an uprising. It shows quite clearly the extent to which Highland dress was seen as a uniform and a sure-fire sign of unity too. The 'Highland Line' – as fabled in popular myth – is the

fault line which cuts Scotland in two. This great diagonal slash cuts from Dumbarton Rock on the river Clyde all the way up to Dunnottar Castle on the coast just south of Aberdeen. Those to the north of this line were considered the true Highlanders, the originators of the kilt and the plaid. Those to the south were lowlanders and – in the eyes of those on the north side of the line – they had no entitlement at all to wear such garments.

THE HIGHLAND LINE

In the 1700s the Highland line became more than simply a figure of speech; it reflected the growing reality of a north–south divide. The ports on Scotland's east coast were of great economic importance: they were thriving with plentiful trade and commerce from abroad. But the very geography of the Highlands contributed to its lack of economic and political clout, particularly when set against that of the lowland areas.

There was always friction between England and Scotland, but this became more apparent in 1707. The two Acts of Union – which together put into effect the Treaty of Union, 1706 – were passed in order to aid the bloody conflict between England and France. It meant that Scotland was to be ruled from Westminster and not Edinburgh. This was not a popular move and the Scottish government relinquished control, but now tartan's identity was even stronger as a definite affirmation of Scottish culture.

PRIDE AND POTENCY

This was the catalyst for the Jacobite uprisings, with Bonnie Prince Charlie collecting his allies from the west coast. It was a time ripe for rebellion. In fact, tartan kickstarted the uprisings.

In 1741 at the Easter Carnival in Rome, Charles Edward Stuart wore a complete tartan outfit. He was coming of age and it symbolised proud links to the clans of Scotland and the Scottish throne. It sent a potent message: the presence of tartan was the beginning of the young pretender's journey to re-establish a Scottish monarchy. So, it's no surprise that tartan has been used in so many dramatic performance pieces on both stage and screen, as well as in print and in art. In 1861 the first colour photo was taken, and it was of a piece of tartan ribbon. Along with colour and history came significant undertones of ambition, conflict, destruction and defeat . . . but then again this was just a photo.

A TARTAN PERFORMANCE

Perhaps Shakespeare's *Macbeth* isn't the ideal starting point to draw tartan into performance, but it offers a flavour of what is to come.

On 28 August 1895, one of the first moving pictures to be produced – by Thomas Edison – was a vision lasting eighteen seconds of *The Execution of Mary Stuart*. Of the 500 or so films shot at this time, it was the first to use special effects,

specifically 'stop trick'. Directed by Alfred Clark, it was also the first film to use trained stage actors in its cast. The lead of Mary, in true Shakespearean tradition, was played by a man. As the axe falls the edit occurs and a mannequin replaces the actor; cutting edge for its time – surely there's a pun there somewhere! The finale of the executioner holding up the severed head is actually pretty gruesome. It marks, as far as I know, the first time tartan appeared on moving film – as part of Mary's dress, in a costume borrowed from theatre.

THE PRIDE OF THE CLAN

Stepping forward a few years, early cinema films retold the stories of old using landscapes and historic locations to give a 'realistic' atmosphere. Film editing was responsible for more continuous narratives, and in 1906 the first feature film was created. Only ten years later a tartan-clad tale hit the screen: *The Pride of the Clan*, starring Mary Pickford. Set on an island off the west coast of Scotland, the story tells of the last chieftain of the MacTavish clan. MacTavish dies at sea, leaving his only daughter, Marget, to assume leadership responsibilities. Her burden is eased by a blossoming romance with Jamie Campbell, but he has a secret past neither of them know about . . . The exaggerated tartan setts and larger-than-life characters are fabulous – and, spoiler alert, Jamie turns out to be the son of an earl. Cue happy-ever-after and closing credits.

TARTAN CAUGHT ON FILM

Next up is 1934's *The Secret of the Loch* – featuring, guess who, the Loch Ness Monster. A batty Scottish professor sets out to prove the existence of the monster with a hot-headed young reporter trying to scoop the story . . . The monster being convincingly played by an iguana and with more tweed than tartan on show. But in 1935, Laurel and Hardy's *Bonnie Scotland* is firmly back in kilts. The comic duo travel to Scotland to inherit an old aunt's estate. It turns out that only a set of bagpipes and a snuff box are left and, in a series of misadventures, they inadvertently sign up into a Scottish regiment and from then on, it's all kilts and pith helmets.

TRUE TARTAN TECHNICOLOR

Post-war saw the advent of colour into cinema, and in 1946 David Niven was cast as Bonnie Prince Charlie in glorious Technicolor. Niven wanted the part so much that he did the audition in full Highland dress to impress Samuel Goldwyn. It's one of the few times you'll ever see David Niven on screen without his signature moustache. The 'epic' was to be filmed on location in Fort William and in studios in London; Niven wanted to escape Hollywood, so this was his perfect chance. Start to end, the film was Royal Stewart tartan. The vibrant red gave the screen an amazing blaze of colour, and, as tartan's first outing in Technicolor, it looked resplendent.

THE HIGHLAND ROGUE

In 1953 Walt Disney swathed the screen with tartan with the swashbuckling adventure of *Rob Roy: The Highland Rogue*, staring Richard Todd as the noble savage. These early colour pieces were *so* clean-cut even the mud looked clean, and it gave the stories an unreal Hollywood veneer. The colours of the cloths were gleaming and their buttons shone bright: it was theatre on the screen. Shot on location in Corriegrennan, extras included soldiers of the Argyll and Sutherland Highlanders who had just returned from the Korean War. Apparently, the soldiers took the fight scenes seriously, using the opportunity to get back at their non-commissioned officers. The *New York Times* described the film as:

A fine lot of fighting among the hills, shooting of rifles, banging of claymores, skirling of pipes and buzzing of burrs, filmed and recorded in color on the actual Scottish countryside. And while Mr. Todd is not precisely the Rob Roy that history records, he is indeed a satisfactory fabrication until a better Rob Roy comes along.

BRILLIANT BRIGADOON

In 1966 tartan graced the silver screen in the guise of *Brigadoon*. The story is of two American friends, Tommy and Jeff, who are stranded in Scotland when their car breaks down. They see a girl, Fiona, and follow her to her home village of Brigadoon, where everyone's preparing for a wedding. The town is under a magical spell, which means it can only appear once every hundred years, and complicated relationship shenanigans follow – in which hearts are followed back to Scotland. Sigh. Tartan is prominent, and the symbolism starts when the friends cross over the bridge to the village and awaken a young girl sleeping under a tartan blanket. She rises from her slumber casting off her protective plaid.

The characters' attire remains untouched by time, allowing the costume designer to give a mid-century touch to the historical. Full-cut romantic shirts, mixed with corsetry and Dior-style skirts, mixed with capri pants and then some 19th-century military tunics: a cocktail of style and colour with a perfect dream-like quality to it. The tartans are unreal too; sett sizes have exploded into massive patterns and colours of no particular tradition. The costume styles of this film are lost in time; in a lot of times, in fact.

STRANGE AND BRUTAL REALITIES

The 1970s saw realism creep back into cinema's Scottish themes. Most particularly, in 1974, *The Wicker Man* explored Scotland's most remote fringes. Edward Woodward starred as a policeman sent to investigate strange happenings on the fictional Island of Summerisle. Deeply disturbing, the film has become a cult classic. Christopher Lee, as Lord Summerisle, does indeed wear the Morrison tartan as part of his Highland costume.

The following year Scottish cinema went from 'sur-real' to 'so real' in *Just Another Saturday* with a stark and brutal look at sectarian violence on the mean streets of Glasgow. Billy Connolly is there in his first 'serious' role wearing tartan in his shirt, or perhaps on his sleeve.

Bill Forsyth, Scotland's 'director's director', produced a series of three films which took Scottish themes away from history and firmly into the here and now that was the 1970s. *Gregory's Girl, That Sinking Feeling* and *Local Hero:* in all these films the costume is of that moment; the kilt and tartan are absent as they tended to be a pastiche rather than a metaphor for Scotland's pride and union. In these communities, tartan was now an accessory, so pushed back that in some instances it feels more like a national burden. You might spot tartan on a Younger's beer carrier bag, and see it as denoting something the character must carry about with them, something that stands out from their everyday attire as both disposable and insignificant.

WHAT'S THE STORY – HIGHLAND GLORY

From the stark realism of a bleak 1970s cityscape, we jump in time . . . To 1986, when tartan, Sir Sean Connery, Scotland and science fiction presented us with *Highlander*. Such a *manly* film with its mix of genres into one action-packed adventure with a soundtrack by Queen, it was a classic from the get-go. Connor MacLeod, played by Christopher Lambert, is an immortal destined to live through the centuries, battling on and on until there is 'Only one!' Here was the return to grand-scale Highland scenery, warriors and battle, but this time with dirt and grit and blood. The film is shot as flashbacks and memories, as pure action adventure, with the philibeg and the great plaid playing as much of a role as the extras. It brought the spectacular natural beauty of the Highlands back in style to the big screen, and tartan in a lesser way.

The 30th anniversary screening of *Highlander* was at the Edinburgh International Film Festival in June 2016. Stewart Christie were lucky enough to dress Clancy Brown, who played the Kurgan, our hero's nemesis. Such a lovely gentleman, we fitted him out in a complete Highland outfit, and so he, along with his son, wore the kilt for the first time on the red-carpet evening – and was actually thrilled to do so!

THE MODERN EPICS

The 1990s saw a return of the epic historical Scottish stories retold for a modern audience. Following in the footsteps of *Highlander*, they pitched a more sympathetic approach to the Scottish plight. Possibly more romance than reality, and not at all my cup of tea (I was never inspired to paint my face blue), they certainly offer a noble vision of Scotland.

Mel Gibson's William Wallace did a sterling job with his accent, unlike the strange accent of Christopher Lambert in *Highlander,* though I still have an issue with the lead man not being Scottish. Liam Neeson at least was Irish! His performance in *Rob Roy* against the arrogant English captain Archibald Cunningham, played by Tim Roth, was well received in a film that's a blend of fact and myth: many characters were pure invention and the plot line's a condensed version of occurrences throughout his whole life.

I do wonder if in the future these films will be seen more as historical fact than fiction, as the myths pile up. But the tartan has the ring of truth about it: Peter MacDonald from the Tartans Authority advised on Rob Roy, suggesting a more grounded approach to creating the romance of the Scottish legends.

OUTLANDISH TARTANS

The next time my feathers were significantly ruffled was with Sam Heughan in *Outlander* (slight swoon). For those of you unaware, this work of fiction from the pen of Diana Gabaldon was made into a serial TV drama of extraordinary sumptuousness. The screen adaptation takes historical occurrences and interweaves them with fictional characters and some steamy bedroom (and non-bedroom) action.

Disclaimer: *Outlander* isn't my usual kind of viewing, and I have to admit to watching it in actual secret. It's truly a reinvention of the ideas Sir Walter Scott laid down all those years ago, with a hint of time travel, and cross-dimensional relationships and offspring. No wonder it's massively popular in America with a certain demographic of the female population. And, yes, there is tartan and plenty of it: peat-stained and sodden, blood-stained and torn.

A special tartan was even created for the series, perfect for those wanting to dress like Jamie Fraser or whose significant others want them to . . . Joking aside, Sam Heughan is a true Scotsman playing a 'true Scotsman', dressed by an expert team of designers who have created a treasure trove of fine outfits lifted directly from historical pieces. I can only imagine the extent of that wardrobe department.

Sam himself visited Stewart Christie before I'd had a chance to watch any of the episodes, so I only knew him by what others had told me. We made him a three-piece tweed suit, which I hand delivered to him in New York 2016, when he was attending the Tartan Week Parade on Sixth Avenue. Sam was the event's Grand Marshall and I have to admit I only realised how huge *Outlander* was stateside when he

invited me to join him on the open-top bus. I looked down onto a sea of fans all vying for his attention.

AN OUTLAW KING

After four series of *Outlander*, it's incredible to report that the world was still hungry for more of the Scottish noble savage. *Outlaw King* starring Chris Pine (great accent, by the way) was a dramatic look at Robert the Bruce and his journey to being crowned King of Scots. Produced by Gillian Berrie and directed by David Mackenzie, *Outlaw King* took a closer

look at the man behind the legend, his personal struggles along with historical events. And, staying true to its time, *there was nae tartan*. The costume was so perfectly designed not only for the period but for the climate; having a dreich and boggy landscape to contend with set the mood perfectly. It was great to see so many Scottish actors appearing in a major Scottish film. Indeed, Nicola Sturgeon highlighted at the film's première the need for investment in Scottish film so it might tell more of the many tales left to tell.

A DRAMATIC QUEEN OF THE SCOTS

To counterbalance all this testosterone, *Mary Queen of Scots*, starring Saoirse Ronan, Margot Robbie and Jack Lowden, graced our cinema screens in 2018. Its costume design was nominated for an academy award; again, faithful to its period, tartan was not present. While the film's historical variations in the plot are to keep the audience interested and the pace flowing, the wardrobe department set the scene to perfection. I was intrigued to learn how all the dark male costumes for the Royal Court of Queen Elizabeth were in fact made out of denim. For me, the patina and look of these pieces certainly took centre stage in a couple of scenes. The two leading ladies blew me away, and I was enchanted to meet Saoirse at the Scottish première. I added tartan to the occasion by lending her a Black Watch tartan capelet to go over her silk Dior evening dress.

A PAIR OF TARTAN TREWS

As it turns out, David Mackenzie has been a Stewart Christie customer for quite a while. For the Scottish première of *Outlaw King* he wore his Stewart Christie tartan trews, purchased when he was 21 (and they still fitted!). I was delighted by this immediate tartan common ground and so asked him a few questions about his films, about Scotland and tartan.

Q&A: DAVID MACKENZIE
Film director

Vixy Rae: What genre of film inspires you most?

David Mackenzie: I tend not to be a genre person and am more interested in films which are not so easily genre-categorisable. But I have a soft spot for the crime and film-noir genres, I love spy stories – and always enjoy good comedy!

Across the films you have directed there are strong themes which challenge traditional notions of relationships. Do you see yourself as creating cinematic truth out of fiction?

I am more interested in grown-up themes in the films I watch and make because they feel more honest and complex. I like films (and books) that feel like they are about something real and truthful. But my kids drag

me to watch the more fantastic material that interests them, and I find myself enjoying that for the first time since I was their age – which is surprisingly pleasant.

Was there any tartan in *Outlaw King*? I looked hard to try and spot some!

In 1307, when *Outlaw King* is set, we don't think tartan as we know it actually existed. But it's very likely that there were some patterns in the weaving of the materials of the time. So, costume designer Jane Petrie and I discussed how to keep the tartan away but hint at it in some of the costumes.

The *Outlaw King* costumes have a real gritty truth to them. Did they impact the way you shot the film?

There are very few references for clothing in this period, but we were keen to make things as close as possible to the time's reality. Jane found some images of clothing that had been preserved in bogs, and these were about the only direct reference. Everything else was rather simplified views from tapestries and drawings, so we had to extrapolate from these. The costumes were a major part of the film in terms of world- and character-creation, but also in terms of how they affect the cast physically and help them channel a sense of the reality of the time.

Some of the grander costumes are quite unwieldy and had a major effect on the way people carried themselves. The wedding and funeral scenes were all about capes that were draped over the shoulders, so everyone had to learn to keep these from falling off. At the time there was not much tailoring, so the costumes weren't fitted in the way we have become used to in the following centuries. For the sake of realism, we avoided the more fitted designed look we could have been tempted by.

How much input did you have on the *Outlaw King* costumes? Do you find it helpful to understand how people can move and behave in certain garments?
I see it as my job to be deeply involved in all the creative decisions on the films I make, so I had a lot of input particularly at the research stages. Jane [Petrie] is super talented, so it was great to work with her and very easy to let her and her amazing team work with as much creative freedom as possible. She's from Dundee and doesn't often get a chance to work in Scotland, so she had a real affinity with the subject matter.

One of my very favourite costumes was a hooded shoulder cape/poncho that Robert and his comrades wore – made of a kind of patterned tweed that could be

seen as a proto-tartan. The tweed was soaked in beeswax, so it was extremely waterproof and ideal for keeping the head and shoulders dry in wet Scottish weather. Beeswax softens at body temperature, so the garments mould to the body and fit in a really great way. They were modelled on the images we used for research, but Jane should be credited for creating our version.

How crucial is the wardrobe in the films you direct? How does wardrobe aid the actors as they embrace their roles?
It's always a special moment when the cast come in to have their fittings because the costume is a major conduit for them finding their character; the way they move with the costumes is a huge part of this. In our case, one of the biggest elements was chainmail and armour. We went for the real thing and this stuff is heavy! When Chris Pine put his chainmail on for the first time, he was immediately transported to the major physicality of what life must have been like for medieval warriors. It doesn't take much running or fighting to get really tired. Our cast were super fit from boot-camp training, but they were still exhausted by the stuff they had to do.

I think costume, hair and make-up combine to complete a sense of a character's physical dimensions. With a film like *Outlaw King*, where we were going back deep into history with very few familiar things to connect with, these elements couldn't have been more crucial in allowing the actors a way into their characters.

Out of the films you have directed which era do you feel most at home with? I guess you don't tend to like futuristic films.

I made two 1950s films back to back a few years ago – *Young Adam* and *Asylum* – and I really enjoyed the atmosphere in them. The 1950s are just modern enough for audiences to have some connection with, but far enough into the past to be exotic. Young Adam was about trying to create a world of post-war austerity in the rivers and canals of the Scottish central belt and I really liked the emptiness this created. You realise our world is so full of things that we have got used to crowded imagery fighting for its space, so it's great to strip it back.

How far does your patriotism extend? Would you include tartan in a film for parody or for more political effect?

'Patriotism is the last refuge of scoundrels and fools,' to appropriate Mark Twain. Across the world we are seeing patriotic ideas being misused by those in power to rally popular support, so one does have to be very careful about patriotism. I am fond of Scotland and feel an affinity to many things Scottish, but I don't want to get misty eyed about it and find myself embarrassed when other people are. Scotland is so enmeshed in myth and legend and sentiment that often it's hard to untangle it from reality. I believe a healthy dose of cynicism is required. One of the key duties I felt in the telling of the Robert the Bruce story was to look for the reality and extract it from the myth wherever possible, to make a real flawed hero out of the legend.

Because it is so striking and instantly associated with Scotland, tartan is almost a natural self-parody already. One of its prime uses when it emerged from the irregular muted plaids of the Highlanders was for military purposes, where identifying uniforms were needed. At the time, the vast majority of the British army was famous for wearing scary red coats into battle, but the Highlanders had one up on them by adding a garishly patterned swishing kilt to strike fear into enemy and subject alike. But to be honest, it's hard to think of a modern use of tartan that isn't in some way a pose.

If you were to direct a remake of *Brigadoon*, **would you make it more like** *Young Adam*? **And would you leave out the tartan?**

I think I would cover it in tartan . . . I might need to think more about this question!

The Mackenzie tartan hails from Ross-shire with dark greens and blues as a base. What tartan garments do you own?

I really like casually wearing a kilt – fortunately the Mackenzie one is not too garish – in a rural environment, walking up a hill, sitting by a fire. My favourite one belonged to my dad and has the texture of multiple repairs. I also have an ancient Mackenzie kilt and trews made for me many years ago by Stewart Christie for more formal occasions and was very happy to wear my trews at the Scottish première of *Outlaw King*.

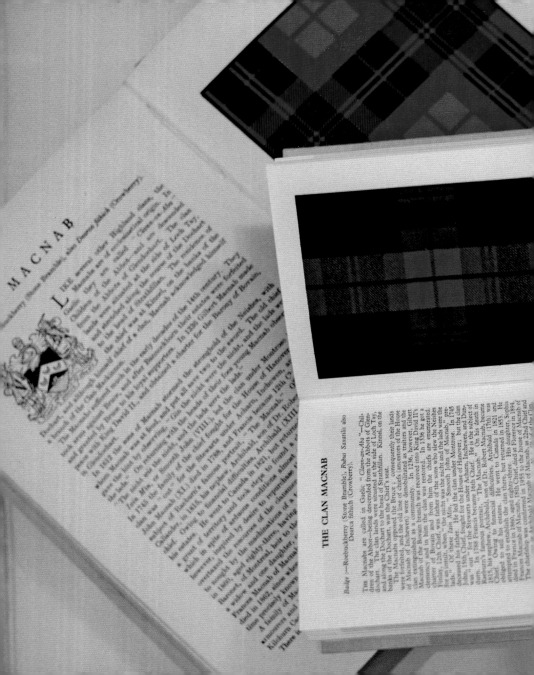

THE CLAN MACNAB

Badge :—Roebuckberry (Stone Bramble), *Rubus Saxatilis* also *Dearca bitulch* (Crowberry).

THE Macnabs are called in Gaelic "Clann-an-Aba" —"Children of the Abbot"—being descended from the Abbots of Glendochart. The clan lands were situated at the side of Loch Tay, and along the Dochart to the head of Strathfillan. Kinnel, on the banks of the Dochart, was the Chief's seat.

The Macnabs opposed the Bruce, consequently their lands were forfeited, and the old line of chiefs was extinguished as traitors and the clan extinguished its branch. In 1236, however, Gilbert of Macnab of Inchewen, were restored. In 1336 he got a charter from... King David II's... the chiefs are enumerated. Finlay 12th Chief, was father of the sons who slew the Neishes... John, 13th Chief, fought under Acham, Inchewen, and Dunardie, and then took part with the House of Hanover, but the clan for the most part was for Montrose. In 1745 for... Smith became 16th Chief. He is the subject of Raeburn's famous portrait. The Macnab." On his death in... Archibald, son of Dr. Robert Macnab, 7th was called upon to resume... He went to Canada in 1821 and settled in France in 1849, and 16th Chief, died at Florence in 1894, daughter, Sophia... clanship to establish the clan... the house of Macnab of Finlay Macnab of... in 1951 to the house of Macnab at 22nd Clan...

REVIVAL

TARTAN

MacNab

Anc green
Anc scarlet
Anc Lindsay red

68 MACNAB

TARTAN RESTRICTIONS

For something to be revived, it has to be near death. And so, in 1747 the Act of Proscription sought to prevent further uprising against the Crown. It was the royalist regime's second attempt to remove a key element of the Highlanders' unity and their clan empowerment by making it illegal to wear certain types of garments.

The common misconception is that the Act was a ban on tartan, but it wasn't, and it didn't apply to everyone. It was a restriction by the English over the Scots and, in some senses, it was more of a disarmament than anything else. It was not put in place to affect the gentry or nobility of the cities, nor was there a restriction on women and children. Instead, it was firmly aimed at the Highlanders and their way of life. The restriction was on 'highland garb'. The meaning couldn't be clearer: these are the clothes of the Highlander.

HIGHLAND GARB

In the 18th century, 'highland garb' referred to:

> 'the plaid, philibeg, or little kilt, trowse, shoulder belts, or any part whatsoever of what peculiarly belongs to the highland garb; and that no tartan, or party-coloured plaid or stuff shall be used for great coats, or for upper coats . . .'

And the punishment for wearing such garb was imprisonment, or for repeat offenders (Rod Stewart comes to mind), banishment via 'transportation to any of his Majesty's plantations beyond the seas and there to remain for a space of seven years'. As an extended holiday, this exile wouldn't have been so bad if it wasn't for the journey, the conditions, the prevalence of disease and the extremely high mortality rate.

TARTAN'S SUMMER OF LOVE

In 1782 the 'ban' was finally lifted with a proclamation sent out to the Highlands. It addressed itself 'to everyman, young and old' and declared that they were now able to play bagpipes, wear a kilt and speak in Gaelic . . . Well, not really but almost. There is fierce debate about whether bagpipes were ever banned, and the speaking of Gaelic certainly wasn't. The Duke of Montrose initiated the Bill in Parliament, something which made him into a local hero. This lifting of the restrictions was more political than simply a change of heart and so 1782 might have felt like the first summer of love for tartan.

There was much celebration; poems and songs were written, but the underlying feeling was perhaps a little more 'meh'. It had now been a generation since tartan was worn in all its glory, and many skills and crafts relating to the cloth had nearly been lost – there had been no practical reason to pass them on. In addition, the Highlands were riven with famine and poverty and so, although tartan was now legally acceptable, many lacked the means to weave or to buy the cloth.

Culloden, too, was now so long ago, as was the time when Bonnie Prince Charlie had found sympathy in France – and his followers had lost faith since even the Pope didn't acknowledge his right to the crown after his father's death. The Prince and his Jacobites were no longer a threat; he was the second-to-last heir to the Stuart dynasty. He was survived by his brother, Henry Benedict, who wanted no claim to a throne at the end of the line (pardon the pun). It was therefore considered a 'safe' time to give something – the wearing of 'highland garb' – back to Scotland.

"

Even today the rules
and formality of
Highland dress are
blurred and defined
by the romance of
the past.

TARTAN FORGOTTEN

The right to wear tartan again came almost too late. By the end of the 18th century, a whole generation had passed and, with the threat of the law and imprisonment hanging over them, people had quickly forgotten the skills necessary to tartan. It was a time of almost unimaginable abject poverty and a dire lack of communication links with the lowlands. And so, it wasn't simply the fact that the techniques of weaving hadn't been passed over, but the know-how which supported and surrounded the craft was also lost.

These losses included recipes for the dyeing of cloth and also the forgetting of the actual patterns of the tartans. The Act of Proscription and the dawn of the Industrial Revolution truly saw the dawn of the dark ages for croft-spun and hand-loomed tartan. Contemporary researchers have difficulty finding much day-to-day tartan from this period, which makes all artefacts from this time so precious.

A DEMAND FOR WOOL

With the purposeful removal of the clan system, life in the Highlands changed for ever. Clan chiefs were now landlords rather than the 'kings' of their own kingdoms. This, combined with the Industrial Revolution, saw the dreadful onset of the Highland Clearances. In brief, the landlords increased rents inexorably, and the working economy of the Highlands suffered terribly. The crofters with their small patches of land could no longer afford the rents – and

so they were 'cleared'. It became more profitable for landlords to use their land for large pastoral farms, for cattle and sheep than to draw rent from those living on it.

Industrial advancements in weaving kept the demand for wool rising. This shift in scale from cottage to mass production impacted upon the availability of different breeds of sheep; hardy sheep were chosen for their ability to survive the Highland weather. Black-faced Linton and Cheviot became the sheep of choice for the entrepreneurial landlords and their farmers. Sheep supplied both wool and meat, and so they generated more profit than cattle. Mass displacement for crofters and clansmen alike was inevitable. Ironically, these crofters would have moved to towns and cities to work in the very factories which had forced them from their land: from the open glens to the dark satanic mills.

TARTAN'S SAVING GRACE

During this time, the Crown decided to raise several Highland regiments for service overseas and – in what could be seen as a morale-boosting crowd-pleaser – the Highlanders were permitted to wear their regimental tartans. Their dress took the form of trews or kilts, and this saving grace for tartan partly aided the cloth's revival. For the Crown, the benefits of this strategy were two-fold: it used the burly Highlanders to police the far-flung corners of an expanding empire thereby removing them to locations where they could cause no more trouble . . . well, to the Crown at least.

THE HIGHLAND SOCIETY OF LONDON

In 1778 The Highland Society of London was formed. As a philanthropic endeavour, it was instigated to preserve and record; it also played a significant role in getting the 'ban' overturned. After which, in 1815, the idea was mooted of approaching all the clan chiefs and asking them to confirm and record their own clan tartans. This was the first time this had been done, and by 1820 around 40 clans had replied and sent the Society samples of their cloth. Surely this exercise was part of a master plan: to ensure the existence of a comprehensive record of tartan.

ROMANCING THE TARTAN

Just as today there is a tendency to romanticise, simplify and de-politicise the Second World War, as the plight of the Jacobites was re-spun in fiction it grabbed the public's imagination. Stories and poems of the warrior shepherds became the fashion, with the likes of Allan Ramsay, James Macpherson and Sir Walter Scott transforming faded memories into popular adventures. Names were changed and circumstances enhanced, but these fictions were all based on real-life events of the period.

Like so much of popular culture, if there is a story there is a poem, and if there is a poem then there is a song . . . and the threads of tartan seem to run through many of them. The archetype of the Highland Laddie became his era's 'bad boy', with his rugged, rough and uncouth reputation promoted by the fiction of the time. While Lord Byron wrote about Lochnagar, Sir Walter Scott was later penning stories of Rob Roy. This majestic Highland empire was inhabited by Scotsmen portrayed as barbarians, but also as irresistible lovers. The allure of this paradoxical image hasn't faded – a glance at films, fiction and advertising shows just how sexy it's still considered today.

THE ALLURE OF THE REBEL

However, as the horrors of battles and conflicts were glossed over, the rebel spirit became a powerful emblem for Scotland as a nation. Those noble fighters from the glens up against insurmountable odds captured the zeitgeist and people hungered for more. So, to coin a phrase, they 'bought the T-shirt' – and wore it. And the T-shirt of the age was tartan.

The imagery of tartan was more important than the truth, and the explosion of tartan fashion that heralded the start of the 19th century had not yet happened. But something was brewing in the mind of a select few in Edinburgh, something which was to cement two separated nations back together . . . or at least that was the plan.

A Royal Pageant in Edinburgh at the beginning of the 19th century would be the first time a monarch from the House of Hanover set foot on Scottish soil. The monarch was King George IV, who had become king at what was then the advanced age of 42. He had been Prince

Regent for over ten years, a decade he passed in debauchery: spending outrageously on palaces, mistresses and partying. George was a close friend of Beau Brummell, the outlandish dandy – and was equally committed to building a reputation for his peacock nature and love of luxury. The pageant was set for the year following the King's coronation: a blatant PR exercise to keep the mood of national optimism buoyant and allow George IV to tour his kingdom and subjects.

THE KING'S VISIT

The Lord Provost of Edinburgh approved Sir Walter Scott's idea and enlisted his help to stage manage the royal visit. It was to be an event the likes of which Edinburgh had never seen before. Scott's house at 39 North Castle Street became operations HQ, and the recently discovered 'Honours' of Scotland were to be the centrepiece of the celebration. The Honours consisted of a lost crown, sceptre and sword of state. All of which had been carefully 'lost' in Edinburgh Castle since 1707. Scott, ever the PR genius, made sure he was present at the 'finding' of the padlocked oak trunk in 1818.

Scott's dream of how the ceremony should look was pure pomp. All would be swathed in tartan, accompanied by bagpipes. He spent his time inviting the clan chiefs – with the proviso that they wear their clan tartan. The history books tell us that 'a lot' came, but 'a few' didn't. And those who did attend, came armed to the teeth: broad swords and 'targets' (shields) rattled to the sound of bagpipes from dawn till dusk.

With his mission to transform even the most gentrified of chiefs into Highlanders, Sir Walter Scott accomplished the best piece of Scottish PR in history. In fact, from this point onwards, the commercial success of tartan was almost guaranteed. From London to Paris and back again, tartan has held its own; whether in or out of vogue, fashion forward or not, from these 19th-century heights it came to occupy its unique place in the aesthetics of fashion.

FIT TO BE SEEN IN PUBLIC

Scott's flagship event was a procession from Edinburgh Castle down the Royal Mile to Holyrood. For it to occur, tradition was reworked and thrust once more into the public eye.

It's a reinvention that forced a sea change: Highland dress became Highland costume. The demands of fashion chose, as always, style over function, as some of the surviving pieces in the National Museum of Scotland show to great effect. We can see how tartan has evolved from

a functional rough cloth to more of a twill weave, and further still into a Saxony fabric almost as soft and light as silk. And, as social occasions demanded more luxuriant cloths, mills met the demand with tartan silk and velvet for truly opulent bespoke and couture garments.

Tartan's place in history was now firmly embedded, which is perhaps surprising given the contemporary cartoons of George IV in his kilt. They show him bizarrely reprobate – an old-enough-to-know-better clubber in a saucy schoolgirl's uniform. Comedic satire at the time, they now look simply grotesque – or maybe that's just me?

A TAILOR'S TAKE

For the procession itself, it's incredible how extensively and extravagantly tartan was used. Not just for kilts but as a complete outfit – and that was just the men. Bias-cut frock coats with belted sashes over the kilt must have been on lots of tailors' work desks in the frantic months preceding the event.

On a personal note, my ownership of Stewart Christie makes me realise how integral tailors were to life at the time. The original company from which Stewart Christie hails is Marshall & Aitken. Founded in 1720, and with a store on the Royal Mile opposite St Giles' Cathedral, Marshall & Aitken would have not only fitted many of the city's residents, but would also have enjoyed a prime spot on the route of the procession itself. To be a Marshall & Aitken tailor would have been quite something!

THE 24TH MACNAB CHIEF

When we talk about clan chieftains, the word still echoes with images of claymores, philibegs and Highland glens. But today they are slightly more genteel; their duties more social than political. It is more about communication and information, about managing the internet rather than feuds. I've always been intrigued by how certain individuals can trace their bloodlines so far back, and I'm delighted to include at least one clan chief in this book. I hope I haven't offended others by not approaching them!

James William Archibald Macnab of Macnab certainly has some interesting stories and links to the early kings of Scotland. The progenitor of the clan was Abraruadh, Abbott of Glen Dochart, rumoured to be the younger son of Kenneth MacAplin, first King of Scots. Angus Macnab was brother-in-law of John III Comyn, murdered by Robert the Bruce in 1306. The Macnabs joined forces with the MacDougall clan against Bruce and, after his victory at Bannockburn in 1314, forfeited their lands and had their royal charters destroyed; these were much later restored by David II of Scotland.

In the 17th century the Clan Macnab feuded with Clan Neish. In the last battle fought at Glenboultachan the Macnabs nearly wiped out the Neishes. Later they fought alongside the Marquess of Montrose at the battle of Kilsyth. Iain Min Macnab gained respect for this victory and was given his own garrison to command at Kincardine Castle. Lord Newark laid siege to the castle, but everyone managed to escape, apart from Iain Min. Captured, he was sentenced to death at Edinburgh Castle.

The 14th chief of Clan Macnab, Robert, married a sister of John Campbell 1st Earl of Breadalbane. This clan connection stopped the Macnabs from supporting the Jacobites. The 15th chief was a major in the Hanoverian Army and was captured at the Battle of Prestonpans in 1745 and held prisoner at Boune Castle for his troubles. The 16th chief, Francis Macnab, was over six foot three; he's the subject of the Macnab of Macnab portrait by Sir Henry Raeburn. Big Francis was a heavy drinker, gambler and womaniser, and is reputed to have died in considerable debt. It's also said he fathered 32 children. Upon seeing two boys fighting over who was the chieftain's son, he broke up the fight, winked at the boys' mothers and said, 'Ah boys, dinnae fight over that, ye both are.'

So, with such a past, we should ask the 24th chief to fill in a few blanks for us.

Q&A: JAMIE MACNAB
The 24th Macnab Chief

Vixy Rae: How far back can you trace your family history?

Jamie Macnab: There is a theory that the Macnab clan dates back to Kenneth MacAlpin, first King of Scots, who defeated the Picts in the ninth century. Kenneth's second son was an abbot; it's speculated that he is who the clan is descended from. In those days, lay abbots were powerful landowners, and *Mac-an-aba* in Gaelic means 'son of the abbot'.

Were the Macnabs locked into any long-term feuds or rivalry with their neighbours?

The Macnabs' enemy was Clan Neish, who they defeated at the battle of Glenboultachan. The Neishes then took refuge on Neish Island in Loch Earn where

they stayed until they were eventually killed by 'Smooth John' and his brothers in 1612 when they slew all of the Neish clan members, other than one boy who hid and who went on to continue the Neish line.

Iain Min, aka Smooth John Macnab, the clan chief during the English Civil War, sounds like quite a bloodthirsty swashbuckler. Is it true he was captured, sentenced to death but escaped on the eve of his execution?

Yes. I believe so. Smooth John is an infamous figure in the clan's history.

The MacNab tartan has many scarlet and crimson tones. Do you know when the cloth was created, and how many variants exist?

I don't know much about its origins, but our tartan is the most attractive of all to me! There are two or three other variations, a green sett which is rarely seen, and an orangey version my father used to combine with the traditional tartan.

The MacNab sett is similar to the Black Watch sett. Have you ever been tempted to create any other variants of the MacNab tartan?

No. I am very happy with our tartan and like combining it with the more orange variant.

Do you know if your family were in attendance at the Royal Pageant of 1822?

My ancestor Archibald Macnab, chief at that time, had lost his lands. He fled to

Canada in 1823, so I expect life was rather fraught for the clan just then. I don't know if any Macnabs were in attendance at the pageant because of this.

Recently, there was a Gathering of the Clans at the Edinburgh Tattoo. Did you attend and did the clan chieftains meet beforehand? (I'm guessing no claymores were involved!)
I represented the Standing Council of Scottish Chiefs, organising all 57 clans who attended the 25 performances. As organiser, I put Clan Macnab forward to attend the press preview alongside Clan Hay in what was effectively the dress rehearsal. Leading over one hundred

Macnabs out onto the esplanade remains one of the highlights of my life.

Is it true the Crown had to grant permission to allow clans to gather en masse within the city walls of Edinburgh?
We had to get special permission for the two or three clans who attended each night to muster in the Great Hall of Edinburgh Castle. I understand this came from Fiona Hyslop, the Cabinet Secretary for Culture, Tourism and External Affairs, who was a great supporter of the event. Brigadier David Allfrey, the executive producer, was the most inspiring person I've ever worked with. I think the clans' participation was deemed a great success!

We made great play on the fact that the Jacobite clans never got into Edinburgh Castle during the Jacobite uprising of 1745 – the Hanoverians fired canons and abuse at them. It was truly a historic event for the clans to muster there for the Tattoo.

As clan chief, are you contacted by those seeking connection with the past? How far afield have the Macnabs roamed?
I'm contacted by Macnabs from all over the world on a regular basis. The clan dispersed and many emigrated well before the Highland Clearances in the late 1800s. Macnabs now seem to be in every corner of the globe. It is a great privilege to meet them. By speaking to me, they are given a living link to their history. A clan is an extended family; connection is a profound experience for Scots who live abroad.

What is your favourite tartan garment?
My father's orange tartan smoking jacket, that Stewart Christie altered for me, is my favourite – but I've not found an occasion to wear it yet. My father used to wear the jacket with traditional red tartan trousers and was always the most colourful person at any gathering. As I understand it, this is how tartan was worn in the past – in colourful clashing varieties, much like how the late Scottish rugby player Doddie Weir wore tartan.

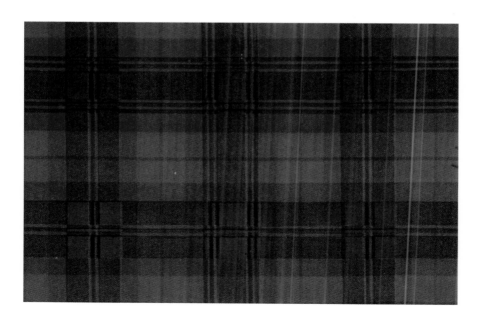

DYEING

Betty's Corner

'Now in her late nineties we didn't pester her, but she would secretly love the notion that we were giggling down by her stream following old recipes.'

A VENERABLE INCORPORATION

'We dye to live!' is the motto of the Incorporation of Bonnetmakers and Dyers in Edinburgh, one of the oldest – it was founded in 1530 – and best subscribed trade incorporations in the city.

The Edinburgh incorporations were early unions and were put in place to safeguard, support and monitor the different trades functioning in the city – such as masons, tailors, blacksmiths and weavers.

Today, the Incorporation of Bonnetmakers and Dyers supports the traditional crafts associated with textiles, provides educational opportunities and rewards textile students in Edinburgh. I have always found their dedication to keeping the past alive utterly inspirational: their passion has spurred me on in my research into the rich trove of stories that tell of dye and tartan and the connections between them.

AN ACCIDENTAL DISCOVERY

Dedicated enthusiasts are slowly nurturing natural dyeing back into fashion, but I thought it important to mention the discovery of synthetic dye, as this marked the end of the era of natural dyes which – as you might expect – had been used for centuries.

In the mid-1800s, industrialisation had a radical, transformative impact upon the UK. As rural people moved to cities, driven at least in part by the promise of better lives and more money, urbanisation swept the country. Cottage industries faltered and fell; crafts and trades that had existed for centuries were lost to mass production,

factories and, in a word, the remarkably seductive new concept of convenience. Many techniques that had always been passed down through the generations began to be forgotten.

Synthetic dye – like so many famous 'discoveries' – was first found completely by accident. At the dawn of the Industrial Revolution in 1856, 18-year-old William Henry Perkin was attempting to synthesise quinine, which, at the time, was used to treat malaria. Perkin's efforts were unsuccessful but, while cleaning up after another failed experiment, he noticed that the remains of his chemical solution had left purple marks in his glass flask. He wiped the flask with a cloth and saw that the chemical stained the fabric purple, giving it a colour that wouldn't wash out.

Young Perkin patented the mixture and opened a dyeworks the very next year. The colour became known as mauveine, inspired by the French word for mallow flower. I can't help but think how ironic it is that nature is the backdrop for the name of something so synthetic. But perhaps people are glad of a familiar reference when new technology is introduced.

Either way, the choice was a wise one. Mauveine's soft delicate name took it to another level and it became a fashion sensation. Until that point, purple was a colour exclusively available to the very wealthy: natural purple dye could only be found in rare molluscs and needed to be extracted in a time-consuming, difficult

way. And so purple became the 'new black' (before black then became the new black in 1861 when Queen Victoria's husband Prince Albert died of typhus). Perkin's discovery revolutionised the world of dyeing for ever, and in many respects changed the world of tartan for ever too. And, as Empire expanded, so did Britain's trade routes, and new dyes of cochineal (red) and pomegranate rind (yellows), Tamil Nadu (indigo) and Manjistha (red) – expensive and rare – from countries such as India, Turkey and China became available, but still only to the wealthy.

NATURAL DYEING: AN AGE-OLD PROCESS

Ever since the Iron Age, people have looked to nature to create colour and vibrancy in their garments. But natural dyeing is not the most reliable of processes. Large-scale fabric production requires a good supply of dye and a continuity of colour – it has to be uniform. This is difficult to achieve with natural dye as the sheer volume of natural ingredients needed to create even small amounts of dye is hard to come by.

And so, the resultant colours depend on a whole set of variables related to the specific ingredients. The climate, growing conditions and location of the plants and animals that supply the dye – and the connections between all these factors – are unpredictable, causing slight (and significant) variations in colour.

MODERN TRADITIONS

When I started writing this book, I thought the origins of tartan and weaving would be a sensible place to start – that this, mixed with the dramatic history of warring clans and rebellions would create a strong image of the cloth's beginnings. I also really wanted to bring the past to life, to take a part of the historical process of creating tartan and try it for myself. In a process that's more 'recreation' than re-enactment, I decided to go back to the roots (and berries) of what goes into making natural dyes – the colours of which have defined tartan since its earliest creation.

REAL MAGIC

Three women in the middle of a field, around an open fire, stirring a concoction brewing in a large pot sounds somewhat Shakespearean. I suppose the kind of chemical alchemy associated with creating natural dyes has a mystery and magic about it, not dissimilar to the eerie witches of *Macbeth*. Certainly, the recipes for old vegetable dyes do sound more like potions than anything else, though the method used to dye fleece is less of a dark art and more of an imprecise science.

THE SHEEP OF ARDALANISH

It was purely by chance that I found my way to the group of wonderful ladies who inspired me to write this chapter on natural dyeing, and who now feel like my extended family. After being asked by many customers for truly authentic vegetable-dyed cloth – the idea is sound, but actually it is a dying art (no pun intended) – I happened across some while on a journey to look at organic cloth from the Isle of Mull.

Ardalanish Farm and Isle of Mull

Weavers is a working farm that specialises in beautiful wool products and grass-fed meat. The weavers at Ardalanish Farm use the authentic colours from sheep's wool to create their patterns in cream and natural black. They also use the leaves from woad plants, madder root and onion to create a spectrum of hues from scarlet to blues and yellows. The Hebridean fleece was once sent away after shearing, but the money paid did not even cover the cost of the shearing. This led to the farm starting to weave their own cloth. The demand is now such that they bring in fleeces from other farms on Mull, who breed Hebridean flocks, Shetland White and Manx Loaghtan.

I can understand why, in this day and age, it's slightly impractical to weave any great quantity of cloth using naturally dyed yarn. It would require such vast amounts of leaves, bark, berries or minerals to create a consistent dye batch. But still it must have been possible. The crofters of the Highlands must certainly have managed it; a philibeg uses in excess of nine yards of cloth, unlike a modern kilt. District tartan was woven from yarn that had been dyed from the colours of the land. Which means there must have been flora in abundant supply, and I suspect that the season for dyeing would have coincided with when ingredients were growing or blooming.

THE COLOURS OF OLD

Colour was obviously important to the early Scots. There are Roman references relating to the Celts' habit of wearing mantles with small squares in many colours. In the kitchen workshops of the past it must have been near impossible to ensure exact colour matches in what would have been so many small batches of wool. This may explain why early checked fabrics contained lots of colours. The colours were probably tones of the same shade, but because of the inconsistency of dye batches they would have perhaps looked multicoloured.

The manufacture of clan tartans with clearly identifiable colours and designs did not come into being until at least the late 17th century with the advent of standardised recipes, imported chemical mordants and larger workshops. Mordants are organic or inorganic compounds which enable the dye colour to be 'fixed' to the fleece or yarn. Until that time, particular colour schemes had much more to do with regionally available plant dyes than with clan associations.

INTO THE DYEING POT

In general, but by no means always, the process of dyeing started with the wool and the plant material being layered in a dye pot. Mordants may or may not be used; wool is highly receptive to mordants because the amphoteric nature of the fibres means it can easily absorb acids and bases with great efficiency. The pot is then filled with water and boiled and stirred until the desired colour is achieved.

Naturally occurring mordants include urine, wood ash, tannins and crab-apple juice. Today, chemical mordants are used – metal salts, alum and cream of tartar. Before the advent of alum, staghorn moss was used as a mordant, and the metal salts could be obtained simply by using a copper or iron vessel as a dye pot, or by adding bog iron or a few rusty nails to the mixture.

The Scots used many plants to dye their wool. In the Western Isles, the slow-growing rock lichens were much-prized dyestuffs, which were used to particular effect in the Harris Tweed industry. The generic term for these lichens is crotal, and it was scraped from the rocks on which it grew in order to produce a wide range of red and brown hues. These lichen dyes also had the added benefit of being supposedly moth-proof. Crotal requires no mordant other than a pre-soaking in urine, hence the distinctive aroma of a genuine Harris Tweed! Until recently, most homes in the Western Isles would have had a 'piss-pot' outside the door and all visitors were expected to donate generously. There was also the unenviable job of going around the local taverns and collecting the urine; the man who did this was called a 'waulker'.

NATURE'S PALETTE

Bearing witness to traditional dye-producing plants, archaeologists in Perth discovered what seems to be a 12th-century dyers' workshop, with the remains of heather, alpine clubmoss, birch bark, tormentil and bracken.

Tormentil, known as blood root, produces a rich red dye. This was used as an excellent leather tanning agent, important in areas of Scotland with few trees. Trees provided bark, and oak bark was a popular choice for tanning. A red dye found in many old tartans has been produced by madder, and it is thought that this was usually imported, as was indigo for shades of blue.

The roots of meadowsweet, picked in late spring or early summer and soaked in urine before boiling in an iron pot, produce an umber colour. Roots gathered in autumn and processed in the same way give black and, if a handful of sorrel is added to the pot, the result is dark blue.

Sorrel, which contains oxalic acid, was frequently added to dye mixes as it helped to fix the dye. The use of an iron pot or the addition of bog iron was important as it contributed the mordant ferrous sulphate to the mixture. This 'kitchen chemistry' is completely fascinating: how can so many slight variables create such differences in tone, shade and colour?

Boiling dock roots in an iron pot could produce dark brown colours. Adding dock

leaves to a dye mixture would brighten or deepen the colours produced by the other ingredients.

Heather was used to achieve yellows and oranges. Using the flowering tops of heather and adding alum could produce richer hues.

Birch leaves and bog myrtle produced a duller yellow. While peat soot, boiled in a bag, was a source of yellowish-brown colours. **Berries** were useful dye sources, and vinegar added to the mix brightened the colours.

White water lily, common in the lochans of the islands, gives a black dye. The roots of the yellow flag iris, dug up after the plant has flowered, will produce a grey-blue colour. This plant was also used in the past to make ink.

THE DYE IN TARTAN

Until I began to think about natural dyeing, I never really saw the dye itself as such a crucial part of tartan. For me, the yarn was the starting point, and then there was the pattern of the tartan itself. But now I can see that an understanding of natural dyes is key to knowing exactly how bright or muted tartan's early incarnations would have been – it can help us visualise what people actually wore before the Industrial Revolution.

AN EXPERIMENT IN DYEING

For my natural dyeing experiment, I wanted a hands-on understanding of the complexity of the process, to discover how the depth of colour compares to today's chemical dyes. So, using some readily available seasonal ingredients, with a team of enthusiastic women around a fire, in a field with large cooking pots, we set to work to recreate two early recipes for two different colours.

BETTY'S CORNER

Waiting for perfect conditions with our Scottish summertime can be a labour of love in itself. Finally, third time lucky. We had an ideal day to undertake our experiment at Garvald Farm in the Scottish Borders. Armed with essential equipment, Alix the photographer, accompanied by our dyeing expert and MA graduate Emily Martin, along with my friend Catherine, who was familiar with the land, we journeyed down to find the perfect nook in which to dye.

The spot we finally chose was aptly named Betty's Corner, after Catherine's grandmother's cousin. Betty was a dyer, and a true woman of nature, who knew more than you can imagine about natural dyeing. Now in her late nineties, we didn't pester her, but knew she would secretly love the notion that we were all giggling down by her stream, following her recipes.

AGE-OLD RECIPES FOR DYEING

As the sun blazed, we undertook the challenge to look at natural dyeing and practice in an authentic manner, using the early techniques. The idea was to see how different vegetation can create different tones and hues on natural wool fibre. We followed some age-old recipes and earlier advice from an incredible group of lady dyers who do this as their hobby.

Alix and I had spent a day with them, to quiz and question and fill up on their practised techniques. They all spin and dye their own wool in and around Dumfries and Galloway. With their wealth of colourful knowledge, we joined them in their monthly spinning session to discuss different processes. They were such a kind-hearted bunch I felt like I had gained a second mother (Liz, please adopt me). I have to thank Liz, Kath, Jan, Pam, Diana and Ruth, for feeding us interesting ideas and fresh scones.

Their fine tales of dyeing with elderberries, onions, pecans, walnuts, crotal and lichens will always resonate with me. I got a real sense of the quantities, what pots to use, and I saw some of their beautiful hand-crafted accessories in an array of natural colours and acid-dyed fleeces.

OH TO DYE

We spent the day at Garvald first foraging and then cooking up the dye lots. Hand on heart, it was my most enjoyable day out in a long time. (I'm planning my next experiment already.) For my experiments, I had some tweaked recipes from the dyeing, ones they had tried and tested, and which achieved the best results.

ONION SKIN DYE RECIPE

- Use the dry outer skins of white onions.
- 50% to 100% of dyestuff to fabric.
- No need to add mordant to the fabric.

Method

1. Soak the onion skins in boiling water for at least eight hours. You need just enough water to cover the skins. Doing this overnight is often the easiest and most time-efficient way.

2. Now pour the soaked skins and water into a designated dye pot and cook on a medium heat for thirty minutes.

3. Meanwhile soak your fabric in warm water.

4. Strain the skins through a sieve and muslin cloth, making sure to squeeze the skins to get all the colour from them. You can now re-soak the skins again in boiling water to get a second extraction colour from them.

5. Now add your pre-soaked fabric to the strained dye liquor and add enough water to cover your fabric.

6. Cook on a medium heat for between forty minutes and an hour, stirring occasionally.

7. Take pot off the heat and allow the fabric to cool in the pot for up to two hours.

8. Remove fabric from liquor and wash until the water runs clear.

9. Remember to save the leftover dye liquor for another dye batch; you can always top it up with extra skins if you want a deeper colour.

NETTLE DYE RECIPE

This recipe is developed from Rebecca Desnos's blog.

- Pick the tops of nettles around spring time and store in a cool dry place.
- 100% dyestuff to raw wool fibres.
- Mordant the fabric as you wish. I chose not to use a mordant for this recipe, which works best with protein fibres.
- Copper modifier – I created mine using old copper coins and vinegar. I left these to sit for months before they developed a green colour. This solution helps shift yellows to green.

Method

1. Cover nettles with cold water and slowly bring to simmering point. Keep stirring and pushing leaves under water.
2. Remove from the heat and let leaves soak for two to three hours.
3. Soak your fabric in warm water while the colour is being extracted.
4. After the nettles have soaked, strain them using a sieve and a muslin cloth.
5. For light to dark khaki results, add small amounts of the copper solution until you see the colour shift. For pale, yellowish green results, follow the next instructions without copper.
6. Slowly bring the liquor to a medium heat (around ten minutes).
7. Add the soaked fabric with extra water to cover if needed and cook on medium heat for thirty minutes.
8. Remove from heat and allow fabric to cool for thirty minutes to one hour.
9. Remove fabric from liquor and wash until the water runs clear.

Q&A: EMILY MAE MARTIN
Slow textile and garment designer

I met Emily years ago when we worked for the same clothing company. I knew of her avid passion for fashion through the ages, and for the skills and knowledge needed to attain a more sustainable approach to clothing. When we first talked about natural dyeing, she filled me with such enthusiasm I had to try it for myself.

Vixy Rae: You first tried natural dyeing as part of your Fine Arts course at Edinburgh College of Art. Was it a success?

Emily Mae Martin: A fellow master's student was also interested in natural dyeing and had already collected flowers from a type of fuchsia for our first test. At the time we were disappointed in the results as the flowers were bright pink but the colour on fabric was a light mossy green. In hindsight, though, it was quite successful, as we're now both well versed in many sad beige dye results!

What areas of clothing and fashion did you focus on throughout your master's course?

Sustainable fashion/clothing was always the goal for me, and I wanted to design a system where I'd thought about every step of the making process, and how each of those can be more sustainable. This naturally meant that I fitted into the world of slow fashion, especially when incorporating traditional craft skills like natural dyeing, quilting and patchwork.

Did you find the course cultivated practical skills relevant to your work today? Were there ideas that you will use in the future?

Not exactly, but the course did provide the time and facilities to explore the skills I chose to teach myself. I feel much more comfortable working with the practical craft skills I mentioned, which means I'm also more confident in my studio practice.

There's a huge craft resurgence at the moment, especially within the sustainable fashion world, so I definitely hope to be using these skills for a few years to come – I always have so many ideas and not enough time! My main aim is to continue gathering information about these skills, particularly natural dyeing, and to pass them on to others in order to keep them thriving.

Were there personal preferences at play in the selection of plants for our experiment?

Of course! Personal but practical choices. One day of dyeing isn't normally enough time, so reliability and availability were key factors.

I love dyeing with onion skins; the colours are incredibly vibrant, plus they have been used for centuries – which just felt like a fun choice when used alongside centuries-old dye methods. We debated a few other plants but then landed on nettles in the hope we could achieve the elusive natural green dye. Plus, this was something I had been wanting to test for a while, so it worked out perfectly.

Which feels right to you – chemical or natural?

Ah! The complicated question. Personally, to explore and understand, I'm always more intrigued by nature. I was raised in Cumbria, and so I have always instinctively engaged with the natural world.

I do think the wider debate on which is better in terms of sustainability is so complex, and also endlessly fascinating. It's definitely not as clear-cut as I initially believed. I would go into it more, but we'd be here for a while – plus I need to get up to date with my research!

We share a passion for slowing fashion down. Do you think you'll make this your focus in future projects?

Absolutely. It is completely tied in to how I make my garments. I really believe that

it adds value to clothing and encourages people to care for their clothes, even if that means they pass them on rather than throwing them away.

What fibres do you usually work with?

I use finished, undyed fabric mostly. Wool, linen, Tencel, hemp and organic cotton, silk organza and bamboo silk are the most common fabrics I work with. I like to source a range of fibres to show variety in texture and colour.

Sustainability is on trend now, but do you see this as a fad or a way of life? Will it be a theme for your future career?

There have been trailblazers for this cause for years now, so I hope it's not a fad. I think referring to sustainability as a trend can be damaging as it should never go out of fashion. The potential for 'green washing' hugely increases when sustainability is perceived as a trend, so my plan is to work against this by creating as sustainably as possible and communicating this honestly. But you're not wrong – it's now cool to be conscious!

Although not always in my immediate circle, there seems to be more people debating the complexities of making sustainable choices, and not just providing definitive solutions, which I find really encouraging.

Can you tell me more about the powders and acid dyes you use?

Chemical or synthetic dyes have been industry standard for years. I'm not hugely well versed in them but I do know they're made from petrochemicals. They often replace natural dyes as they are practically superior in almost every way – better colour saturation, a huge variety of colours and also better light, wash and rub fastness. Plus, you get these results from a small amount of powder, rather than large amounts of natural dyestuff. These colours are also easier to replicate – correct colour matching is of huge importance within the larger industry.

What will your next project be? Do you have a new palette or plant in mind?

I'm definitely planning a quilted jacket or two for myself. I'm wanting to design more garments using undyed fabric to make the colours really pop, plus it will help reduce dye materials and time.

I never really have a palette in mind – I like nature to dictate this for me. However, I am planning to try and phase out my use of alum as a mordant (fixative) and test my avocado, onion and black tea dyes as a mordant instead.

INSIDE

TARTAN
Royal Stewart Hunting

Anc green
Anc blue
Black
Anc yellow
Anc scarlet

A ROYAL BAN

It is hard to believe that in this day and age there are explicit restrictions on tartan. This doesn't mean there is still a ban, or that there is such snobbery that there are social restrictions on wearing the cloth. Rather, it is an actual fact that one particular tartan, the Balmoral tartan, is restricted to members of the royal family and the royal household. This grey, red and black tartan – designed by Prince Albert in 1853 – can only be woven under permission from the royal family and only for use by the royal family.

The 1822 Pageant for King George was the catalyst for our modern obsession with tartan, but at first it seemed short-lived as the king soon grew tired of tartan garb. However, his niece Victoria was to form an intense and lasting love for the Northern Kingdom. Her passion for the Highlands – and for all things Scottish – endured throughout her life, signifying the ease she felt in Scottish company, landscapes and culture. Victoria's visit to Scotland – with her beloved Albert in 1842 – marked the start of a lifelong love affair with the country and its people.

VICTORIA & ALBERT

The royal couple had been married for two years when they journeyed north to be greeted at each port of call by the local chieftains. Of course, Victoria and Albert's experience of Scotland was privileged – it was curated, determined by their status, wealth and power. But still, there was a

lack of grandeur to these receptions, which meant the two travellers felt they had been treated to honest, authentic spectacles.

Queen Victoria was most taken with their visit to Taymouth Castle. Upon receiving the couple, pipers and clan chiefs presented their sovereign with scenes which hadn't been seen since feudal times. They gave the young queen a performance which was symbolic and romantic.

DIARY OF A ROYAL VISIT

A Mrs Maule, the wife of a local MP for Perthshire, was a guest at Taymouth Castle and kept an account of the royal visit at the time:

7 Sept: Awoke at 7 with 'Hey Johnnie Cope' from the pipers at the camp. A misty morning, very warm, all anxious and in expectation of our Sovereign Lady's arrival . . . The village of Aberfeldy was very gay with 2 arches of heather erected, also one at the entrance of Lord Breadalbane's property . . .

At 10, people in the park beginning to collect and the mist rising gracefully from the hills. The flags flying, birds singing and the hum of voices . . . From one o'clock we began to see people flocking into the Park, all the ladies with Tartan in scarfs or ribbons. 50 of Sir Neil Menzies' tenants clad in their Tartan joined the rest in front of the house . . .

Her carriage and 6 other carriages followed. Lord Breadalbane at first stood in front of his splendid Highland Guard of 200 men and then having made a bow, bonnet in hand, he came round and assisted the queen to alight and came up stairs to the drawing room where we were all waiting to receive her.

BY THE QUEEN'S ACCOUNT

Queen Victoria's diaries echo these sentiments, as she was introduced into a curious world unlike that of London or the rest of England.

We reached Taymouth, situated in a valley surrounded by very wooded hills – most beautiful. At the gate we were met by a guard of Highlanders, Lord Breadalbane's men . . . Lord Breadalbane himself was in Highland dress (all wear the Campbell Tartan) & stood at their head . . . There was a great crowd, & the whole scene, with the firing of guns, to add to its impressiveness, was the finest sight imaginable, & seemed like the reception in olden Feudal times, of the Sovereign by a Chieftain. It was truly princely & romantic.

DEAR PARADISE

Two years later the couple returned and stayed at Blair Castle; this was followed with a tour of the Outer Hebrides on the Royal Yacht three years after. The next year, they leased Balmoral and, as their love and connection with the Highlands grew, in 1852 they purchased the estate and set about their grand scheme of remodelling.

'This dear paradise,' as the young queen called it, was redesigned by Aberdonian architect William Smith, who drew his inspiration from classical Scottish baronial style. The exterior was created for their functional needs, while the interior was the sole design of Prince Albert. It was less a stuffy palace and more a regal hunting lodge; styling as relevant and fashionable today as it was in the 1860s and onwards.

THE BALMORAL TARTAN

Balmoral's interior was brought alive by the use of textures and patterns; it was cheerful but at the same time cosy and reflective. It became Victoria and Albert's haven, a place for them to escape to, and was a sanctuary to Queen Elizabeth II. Tartan greets you throughout the property, with Royal Stewart and Hunting Stewart used for the carpeting, while Dress Stewart is the pattern of choice for upholstery and curtains. Artistic impressions show how the tartan is mixed with patterned chintz to create a baronial hunting lodge with what was then a modern twist.

As mentioned, Prince Albert himself designed the Balmoral tartan. There also existed a pattern called Victoria, which was based loosely on the Royal Stewart sett. In the archives at Stewart Christie & Co. is a swatch of the first batch of the cloth, created in around 1850. It uses the dark and light greys of the local granite and these are interlaced with a strong but subtle red to make a very distinctive cloth. Many seek it, but few are allowed to wear it.

MEMORIES OF A NEW DESTINATION

The Victorian era marked the beginning of the tourist industry for Scotland. As new railway links encroached from the south and more shipping routes came northward, it became easier for visitors to access the hallowed lands of the north. This in turn created a need for the souvenir, but these were true souvenirs – memories – of Scotland: Scottish made and not, forgive me, the imported tat we are swamped by today.

For early tourists who weren't so keen on the wearing of tartan, there was a plethora of souvenir items to choose from: from silk-covered books to jewellery boxes, from fine china to tea caddies. As the tartan trend swept the nation it was wryly noted that this was the first time in a few hundred years a monarch had come from London to spend so much time in Scotland, without invading, colonising or otherwise disrupting! Likewise, the locals and the clans welcomed visitors – royal and non-royal – on the basis of a mutual respect for their way of living.

For travellers of the time, a Scottish visit was more exploration than a simple day trip. It was only with the advent of the steam railway that Scotland became truly open to the middle classes. Before this, it was a case of coach and horses, and the lack of 'roads' in the Highlands made this type of travel extremely slow and hazardous. In 1876 Dr Samuel Johnson took a grand tour of Scotland and the Islands. He commented:

It need not, I suppose, be mentioned, that in countries so little frequented as the islands there are no houses where travellers are entertained for money.

So not only was the journey harsh, but when you arrived there was often nowhere for you to stay. A little later than Johnson, another travel writer described how his journey to the 'frightful country' was made extremely difficult:

For two principal reasons, one of geography, and one of culture. The physiography of the Highlands made travel arduous and slow.

This latter was written in 1974!

THE ROYALS IN SCOTLAND

Queen Victoria's attitude seems to have been passed down through the generations and Scotland remains a place where the royal family can be a 'family' without the unwanted intervention of the press or the public. The late Queen Elizabeth II loved the countryside around the Balmoral estate and often walked the hills accompanied by a single bodyguard. There is a delightful story of Her Royal Highness being stopped by an American couple who asked her the best route to Balmoral. Not immediately recognisable in her headscarf and glasses, they went on to ask if she was 'from around these parts' and if she had met the queen? The lady in the headscarf politely replied she was but that, as yet, she had never met the queen!

King Charles inherited the neighbouring estate of Birkhall from the Queen Mother. While attending Gordonstoun on the Moray coast, he frequently visited his grandmother at Birkhall, preferring to spend his weekends there than at the school. And so, the estate became his second home, and it remains one of the king's regular residences: a home more akin to a hunting lodge than a palace.

"
There are few secret little corners left in the world where a son has followed his father's footsteps with consideration and passion for the craft.

A PRINCELY TARTAN

The Duke of Rothesay is an outstanding advocate for tartan. Each time I have met him (bar one) he has been sporting a kilt. His current favourite pattern is an old and rediscovered one – the Prince Charles George Stewart tartan, which in my opinion really suits him! It's incredibly stylish, and if you visit Dumfries House in the Borders, you'll see a portrait of him in a commanding position at the entrance.

The production for this tartan was undertaken by the Andrew Elliot mill in Selkirk, which is very much a mill truly (and happily!) stuck in Victorian times, and only a stone's throw along the road from the ultra-efficient and modern Lochcarron mill.

The Elliot archive room is home to a length of this princely tartan, kept from the original batch woven. The mill's current owner, Robin Elliot, is proud of this royal connection and how his mill weaves the cloth to create the King's favourite kilt. He was kind enough to let us photograph the workings of the mill and to answer a few of my questions.

he set up his own business as an avenue for his designs. Initially he ran the business from home, and had his fabrics woven in Galashiels, then in 1972, he set up, with my mum Margaret, his own in-house weaving mill at Forest Mill, in what was the old yarn store of George Roberts & Co. a large-scale weaving mill which had ceased trading by the late 1960s. It's from this building that we still operate today.

We have some beautiful pictures of your working looms. Can you tell me about the different types and what they can do?
We have six working looms – four broad-width on which we produce the majority of our fabrics, and two narrow-width looms on which we produce single-width cloth. They are Hattersley Dobcross shuttle looms, which can weave up to seven colours. They have four shuttle boxes at each side, and as you always have to have an empty box to receive a shuttle, seven is the maximum number of colours we can weave. For example, the Hawick tartan has seven colours.

The four broad-width looms date from 1955 and 1960. We produce all of our full-width tweeds and tartans, plus our large blankets, and most of our commissioned fabrics on these looms. The two narrow-width looms date from 1928, and on these we produce our single-width tartans – for anyone ordering just a single kilt length or for any kilt material needed to be specifically woven that way, as well as our small blankets and any commissioned items such as wide scarves or stoles.

Q&A: ROBIN ELLIOT
Owner, the Andrew Elliot Mill
Vixy Rae: How did the mill come about? Has it always been in the same location?
Robin Elliot: My father Andrew set up A. Elliot (Fine Fabrics) Ltd in 1965. He'd been in the industry since leaving school in the early 1940s, as a designer, first working for Wilson & Glennie's in his hometown of Hawick, then moving to Port Laoise in Ireland to work for Irish Worsted Mills.

He returned to the Borders in 1960, settled in Selkirk and set up as a freelance designer, working with mills in Ireland, northern England and the Harris Tweed industry. But his designs were the property of the mills he was contracted to, and so

Do you feel you have followed in your father's footsteps with the same passion?

Absolutely, and although I have childhood memories of the mill, and did occasional work at the mill during school holidays, I didn't come into the business straight from school. When I finished school in 1988, I started a course in accountancy. However, I failed the first year and took a job in the mill – still with no intention of being involved in the management of the business – until the summer of 1990. I left Selkirk for a couple of years, living in Glasgow and Edinburgh, and working in any job I could get, before I moved back to the Borders and went back to college.

It was then I decided to get involved in the business. I started an honours degree in textiles at the college in Galashiels in 1992 and, while working at the mill during any spare time and holidays, graduated in 1996 and came into the business full-time. Next, I became a director and shareholder, and I worked very closely with my father up until he passed away in 2009.

My passion for the business, and the satisfaction I get from our work, is key. As I say to a lot of people, part of what I do is make sure Dad's name remains 'above the door'. Although I am the MD and the only one driving the business forward, I never lose sight of what he achieved and of what the name means.

You were telling me about a very special commission you undertook. What was so special about this tartan?

In 2015, I waas asked by the Scottish Tartans Authority to weave a kilt length of the Prince Charles Edward Stuart tartan, one of very few patterns that have been woven, unchanged, since the mid-18th century.

The sett, in this case was based on a specimen woven around 1790 by William Wilson & Son of Bannockburn and, working with the Authority's Chairman and Head of Research and Collections, we matched the shades to the traditional natural dyes of the period and incorporated a traditional herringbone selvedge, a feature commonly found on rural Highland cloth in the 18th century.

The Scottish Tartans Authority presented this tartan to HRH The Duke of Rothesay in early 2016, and it is so pleasing to see His Royal Highness wearing a kilt made from the fabric on a regular basis. What a wonderful endorsement for the quality of our cloth!

I found it so refreshing to be at a mill where both tartan and tweed are woven. How do you see the differences between them?

The main differences between tartan and tweed are in the design and feel of the fabrics. In design, tartans are symmetric for

the most part, have very distinct patterns (which makes them easy to register) and are mostly woven in fine worsted wool. Having said that, some mills do produce qualities [of cloth] in synthetics, and we've also produced, as have others, tartan in other qualities of wool, which give the cloths more of a tweed 'feel'.

The patterns we produce in tweeds can vary from very simple solid colours, windowpane checks, herringbone or houndstooth cloth, to quite complex multi-colour checks. Virtually all tweed is woven using wool in some quality or other. Most of the wool we use is merino (from Australia and New Zealand), which is a softer finer quality than our native breeds. This allows us to produce softer tweeds for apparel wear, and for use in home interiors and soft furnishings. We do use some indigenous wools, but only if the yarn spinners who

supply our yarn have those qualities available. These can include British wools such as Cheviot, Jacob and the like, and Irish Donegal yarns.

Yarn is a precious commodity. How do you recycle any leftovers? Does your mill create sustainable cloth?
Whatever yarn we have left over from weaving will always end up either being held over for further orders or being worked away into our Ecology throws. We weave this unique range of throws using both leftover and discontinued yarns that I buy at discount prices. While I'm aware that some mills produce 'random rugs', I don't think anyone produces rugs as unique and individual as the ones we do. No batch that we produce is the same. They are very much hand-woven, with the weaver selecting particular colours, and often weaving no rug

the same within a batch of, say, twenty rugs.

I'd absolutely say that we create sustainable cloth. We are keeping alive and maintaining a particular method of manufacturing, which has in the main died out. All of our fabrics have clear provenance and branding, and we have a clear story behind our business and our brand. We use a clear source of yarn supply, and all of our cloths are finished locally, with a completely natural process of scouring (one could say in the natural soft local waters) and cloth processing.

Do you work with many fashion houses or merchants to create specific patterns and weights of tartan and tweed?

Most of the tweeds we weave are sold through cloth merchants, including exclusive ranges of different weights and qualities of tweed, as well as our own range of tweeds. We weave specific patterns for textile designers for their clients, and we undertake private commissions for clients wanting a specific tweed or tartan. Some of this work involves designing the particular tweed or tartan based on the client's story or brand, rather than simply producing the client's own design.

Given the nature of your looms and your ability to weave authentic-looking cloths, have you recreated any historical fabrics?

We have worked on a number of projects over the years to recreate historical fabrics. Most of these are done in collaboration with Dr Ian Dale of Angus Handloom Weavers, who produces authentic fine linen, silk and jute fabrics on jacquard looms. He would supply those fabrics for a project, and we would in turn supply the matching woollen or worsted fabrics.

One of the largest projects we worked on was for the refurbishment of the Great Tower at Dover Castle in 2009, where we supplied over 700 metres of fabrics for wall hangings, floor coverings, bed drapes and throws, chair backings and seating. We have woven cloth for the Globe Theatre in London, the V&A Museum (for the Great Bed of Ware), Kew Palace, Osborne House, Anne Hathaway's cottage at Stratford-upon-Avon, and many others. Back in the 1980s we even wove a special wool interior cloth for Dolly Parton to be used in her house at Martha's Vineyard.

And the killer question: tartan or tweed?
Our business is about 75 per cent tweed, 25 per cent tartan. Tweed is what we've always been renowned for. We have our own range of stock tweeds, but we don't do a stock range of tartans: we only weave tartan for specific orders and clients. However, in recent years, we have become renowned for our special tartans and for the bespoke – one might say artisan – way we produce our tartans. We are also one of the few mills to weave all our tartan, every single inch of it, in-house – something not many artisan weavers can lay claim to. Although they try!

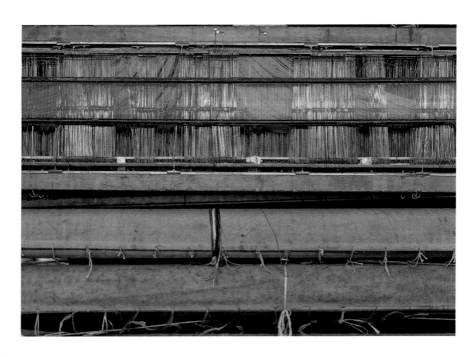

OUTSIDE

Skye

Brown
Light grey
Purple
Green
Light green
Dark green
Hunting green
Grey
Olive green

'NEVER LET THE TRUTH GET IN THE WAY OF A GOOD STORY . . .'

Is an adage that Scottish history seems to have taken to its heart. Thanks, Mark Twain! To me, it feels as if perceptions of our history are based around an 'embroidered truth', or perhaps some colour has been woven into the facts to form a vibrant and steadfast pattern, and then more layers have been added, so the tone is altered for another generation. Something strong and vivid is at the core, but as it shifts and interweaves, pinning it down proves tricky. This motif reflects the evolution of tartan as its status as the cloth of a nation ebbs and flows through time.

So where would we start if we were to look at tartan simply as a fashion fabric? The 1970s? The 1870s? Hard to put an exact point on it; it's a bit like asking, 'When did fashion become fashion?' The history of the cloth indicates that it starts with the 'right' to wear tartan. Tartan includes lots of colour and complex patterns, both of which take time and money to create, and so it was originally reserved for the upper levels of Highland society. As a tailor, this makes complete sense to me; only the heads of the clans and those in their immediate family would have been afforded the courtesy of wearing the family colours.

THE SAME WOOLLEN STUFF

Although tartan is seen throughout history as a very masculine fabric, there are clear records from the early 17th century of its use by women. A visiting nobleman to Edinburgh, Sir William Brereton noted in 1636, 'Many wear plaids, which is a garment of the same woollen stuff where saddle cloths in England are made, which is cast over their heads, covers their faces on both sides, and would reach almost to the

ground, but they pluck them up and wear them cast under their arms.'

Sir William goes on to talk about the 'earasaid' or 'arisaid', which the drawings from this age tend to depict as a really large shawl. In some respects, this echoes how women might choose attire that covers the head and is then wrapped across the face for protection or modesty. On the Hebrides, the women of the time possess a particular elegance, using this garment to indicate their marital status. To delve a little deeper, the married ladies would wear the 'earasaid' along with a '*breid caol*' or slim neckerchief; the single ladies would wear a '*stiom*' which was more like a headband ribbon.

It seems it would have been the norm at least until the middle of the 18th century for ladies of the Highlands to wear these 'plaids' created from coarse wools with a twill weave. The plaids were, as Sir William points out, used for furnishings, functional blankets and outer garments. An impressively multi-functional cloth, with its various purposes derived from necessity, the plaid could be heralded as the functional fashion of its time.

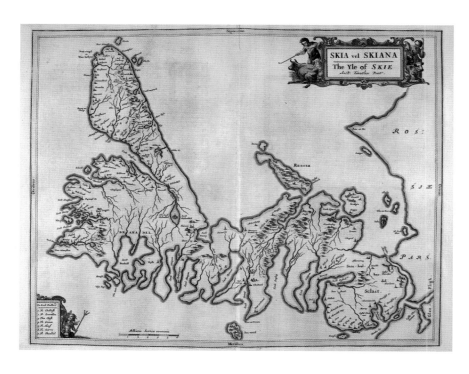

HEARTS AND MINDS

Historically speaking, nobility or royalty have tended to lay down the fashions of each era; that is, until the democratising advent of moving pictures and popular musical trends. So, back in the 17th century, finer woven cloth was a clear status symbol. But as we move into the 18th century we see a shift as techniques evolved and the first and second Jacobite uprisings happened. The first was quickly quashed, but the second left discontentment throughout all levels of Highland society. At this point tartan was used as a poignant reminder that rebellion still filled the hearts of many.

This stance can be seen in portraiture, with artists such as Richard Wilson, Jeremiah Davison and Sir Joshua Reynolds depicting landmark figures of the time in tartan and full Highland attire; in silent but obvious defiance of the union of the two countries and against English rule. Subtle details in some pieces show a white rose as a symbol of direct support for the now exiled Prince Charles Edward Stuart. This was the first time that tartan was portrayed as a rebel cloth, a subversive act against the Hanoverian regime which would govern the nation.

FROM INSURGENCE TO OBEDIENCE

Tartan fast became a statement piece: once worn by the rebel it now became society fashion. By 1765 prominent pro-Hanoverian supporters were proudly wearing the cloth in their portraits. So, although the reasoning behind the wearing of tartan shifted, it survived the prohibition. The ban was for Highlanders in their 'garb' and didn't affect those of 'notability'. By the 1750s most women would wear their 'plaids', too, and you were noted by the type of fabric you wore. High society wore silk and woollen tartan garments, complete with silk linings, and while this trend lasted in the countryside, in the cities the plaid fell from grace to be replaced by silk or velvet cloaks.

TARTAN PEACOCKS

It wasn't until Sir Walter Scott's infamous reinvention to celebrate King George IV's visit that tartan once again became the height of fashion. As the gentry and nobility busied themselves peacocking to outdo each other with the most notable, head-turning and flamboyant outfits for the royal visit, they created a tartan frenzy. It was a milestone: the first time tartan was an actual 'trend'. A few of the most beautiful examples of these outfits are held in the National Museum of Scotland's archive, donated by some of Scotland's clans who attended the event. Like so many of the high-fashion pieces found in museums, these extraordinary tartan ensembles survived thanks to their very decadence: worn very rarely and handcrafted from sumptuous silks and silk velvets, they weren't subject to everyday wear and tear.

Just like peacocks, the men's outfits are more flamboyant than the ladies'. Bias-cut tailcoats, with leg o' mutton sleeves and deep gauntlet cuffs, matched with finely detailed funnel-neck waistcoats and finished with a short kilt – plus, in some cases, a sash for good measure! So many layers and so many directions of cut, creating an outfit which would certainly turn heads and, depending on your choice of tartan, might become outrageous enough to turn stomachs too!

FIT FOR A PRINCESS

If we jump forward to the 1860s, Highland Style next comes into vogue with a young princess's love affair with Scotland. One of the archive pieces in the National Museum of Scotland, which would be incredibly expensive to recreate today, is a silk tartan velvet full-length dress with lace trim and white satin band. It sounds pretty standard until you realise that the silk velvet would cost in excess of £300 per metre if it were plain. The process of making velvet is like creating a cloth sandwich, with two layers of pure silk being joined with silk pile, then the whole piece being cut in two to create a fine soft pile and two identical pieces of cloth. From a tailoring perspective, the process is mind-blowing, as some areas of the fabric have sections which just show the silk undercloth with no pile on it at all.

To put such extraordinary craftsmanship into context, I recently tried to source silk velvet for a very special client at his own request. My journey took me to Lyon where some of the world's finest silks are still woven, and so my own experience tells me that a dress in silk velvet tartan in this day and age would be something truly expensive. Back in the 1820s, such a gown could only have been the statement piece for the social elite.

TARTAN, TARTAN, EVERYWHERE . . .

With Queen Victoria and Prince Albert set on decorating Balmoral in their own Scottish Baronial style, it wasn't long before check was everywhere – garments, furnishings and everything in between. Up and down the country, tartans were created to capture this interest and you no longer needed to be entitled to wear the cloth: it was for everyone. The fashion extended into tourist fodder and souvenirs, with Mauchline boxes produced in tartan . . . and soon tartan truly was everywhere.

I can't help but think this ubiquity divided Scottish hearts then as now – there's a joy in the national cloth becoming so widespread and, at the same time, there's a loathing for the diluting and sanitising of one's past and one's heritage. Not to mention the cultural appropriation punch in the gut of seeing it worn by the English.

The premature demise of Prince Albert marked an end to this exuberant tartan mania. Queen Victoria lost the love of her life, and all the colour drained from her world. As the nation joined her in grief, a mourning tartan was created using black and the white basis of dress tartan. Thus, there was a shift away from bright colours to a more sombre mood.

"

Representing Scotland at Miss Intercontinental in
Sri Lanka was definitely not my typical day as a dental
student. I visited Stewart Christie & Co. at their Edinburgh
workshop with the hope of embracing my Scottish
heritage and celebrating my family tartan. It became a
timeless experience, which seamlessly married a wealth
of heritage knowledge with a fresh, current take on
fabrics and cuts. The outcome was an elegant
made-to-measure piece that I loved wearing on an
international stage.

– ABIGAIL GLIKSTEN

ROYAL CONNECTIONS

Royalty maintained its love of tartan and its Highlands links, but in the earlier years of the 20th century the advent of a new age meant that tartan was reserved for military and formal attire. It wouldn't sweep the nation in such a craze again! For Stewart Christie, its links with royalty begin in modern times with King George V, grandson of Queen Victoria. As we're now in the age of photography, evidence of his love of Scotland and 'traditional' Scottish dress can be seen quite readily. But still it was simply not the done thing for a royal to wear a kilt in England.

All Stewart Christie's records regarding King George V show a monarch with a sincere respect for the clothing he wore in Scotland. He took a traditional, understated look, one which held a timeless elegance and didn't push any boundaries. He instilled this respect for Scottish traditions in his children; maybe the instinct for trend-setting skips a generation or two, or perhaps Edward VIII, Duke of Windsor had a natural penchant for style. Certainly, the royal line did a great deal to support and promote tartan.

The Duke of Windsor shared a passion for the cloth with his great-grandmother, Victoria, and he was never afraid to mix and match patterns. He often sported extremely baggy plus-fours in Glen Urquhart check, matching them with Argyll sweaters and tartan hose. His style was to mix colour on colour with pattern on pattern, but he always seemed to keep within the realms of taste, never gaudy or overstated, just

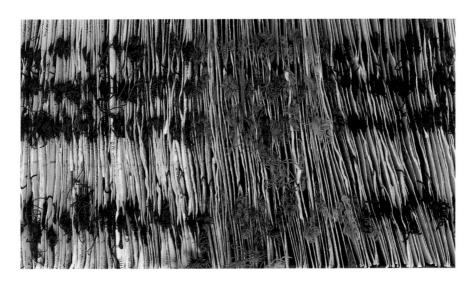

well put together. In fashion terms, an inspiration to those of his time, and to future generations too.

The Duke of Windsor had the right to wear Royal Stewart, Hunting Stewart, Rothesay, Lord of the Isles and Balmoral tartans, and, unlike his forefathers, he didn't restrict himself to wearing tartan only in the Highlands, thus making it aspirational again. One of my favourite outfits of his is a MacDonald Lord of the Isles two-piece double-breasted suit. It was tailored for evening use but still pushed the boundaries of what was acceptable. The tartan is three shades of green with a white accent, not necessarily formal until cut into a double-breast with a high waist.

The only other person in his life who shared such a passion for colour and pattern was the Duchess of Windsor, Wallis Simpson. One of the auction pieces at Sotheby's in the Windsors Collection was a Dior-designed dress cut from the Balmoral tartan. Simply cut and effortlessly stylish, with checks perfectly matched, it must have caused some controversy at the time . . .

With the duke's transatlantic connections and his preference for having his trousers tailored in New York and his jackets tailored in London, it seemed logical for the Ivy League to embrace tartan as part of the 'preppy' or 'Wasp' look. But the advent of the Second World War meant that brightly coloured and heavily patterned fashion took a pause. Tartan remained the garb of the military, but in such dark, austere times the rationing of clothing meant that tartan was seen only in generational pieces rather than in current fashion pieces.

TARTAN ROCKS AND ROLLS

Post-war saw a boom period, particularly in America. The rebel cloth reinvented itself as part of the fast-emerging youth culture and took its place in the world of rock 'n' roll. Tartan sett size was reduced and used for shirting; colours shifted to be used in suitings. Bill Haley rocking around the clock in his drainpipes, shawl-collared tartan suit with his slicked-back hair and winkle-picker patent shoes heralded the look of the rebel era. It was one with a smarter edge, polished and sharp, dramatic and vibrant, an ocean away from the grit and roughness of the Scots. I see the Beach Boys in their matching plaid shirts with their neat haircuts, tanned skin and beaming smiles; I can't see any signs of rebellion, just eager, sunkissed looks. Even the original rebel without a cause James Dean wore tartan, but subtly: on the inside of his red Harrington jacket.

Twinsets, bobby socks, a high ponytail with either cropped tartan capri pants or mid-length skirt looked to be the female all-American teen uniform, but in Europe, as fashion designers directed trends for the wealthy, music did the same for the youth.

Christian Dior and Coco Chanel both used tartan within their collections of the 1950s, but as individual pieces using the structure of the pattern to give their defining

"

Vivienne Westwood reinvented tartan in the 1970s and into the 1980s with her irreverent, but massively stylish, bondage trousers and suits. Malcolm McLaren and the Sex Pistols rocked her clothes, looked stunning and seriously dangerous. Punk not only had a seismic impact on music, but also on fashion and design. I was a little too young, but loved it from afar . . . I did have some cheap and nasty bondage breeks as a teenager, but I've always wanted a quality pair. Thanks to a length of tartan I inherited from an uncle and Stewart Christie's tailoring skills, I now have some, love them too. Punk as f**k!

VIC GALLOWAY,
BBC broadcaster, author,
journalist and musician

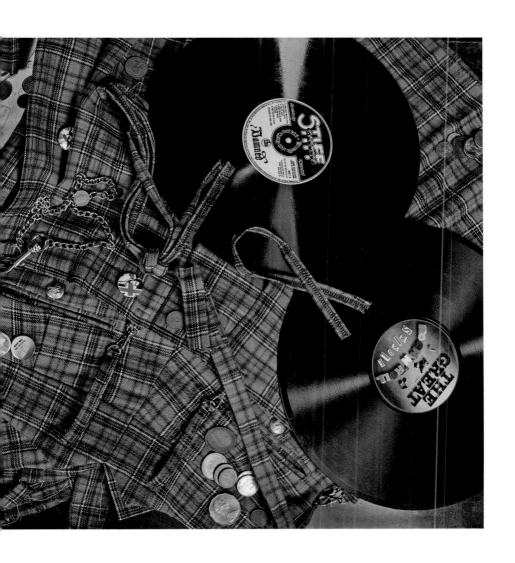

cuts more edge and drama. Dior's New Look really lent itself to tartan. The heavily fitted top and the slim waist flowed into a wide flared skirt. In most cases the Dior dress would have a bias-cut circle skirt with a straight-cut top, giving movement and drape to the lower regions of the body with rigidity and form to the bodice and bust.

TARTAN CHECKS INTO THE FUTURE

The 1960s saw the defined lines of structured garments for women relax. Hemlines came up and the feeling in Britain was one of economic growth with music and street fashion creating the direction for the trends. Prosperity and more disposable income allowed fashion that was accessible, faster paced and youthful. Ready to wear, off-the-peg clothing became more and more popular. Synthetic fabrics delivered more vibrant colours and tartan was an obvious direction. Mary Quant, Biba, Pierre Cardin and Yves Saint Laurent were at the forefront of 1960s design and tartan somehow seemed to fit into their vibe of 'space race' futuristic designs and cuts. In some cases, the colours became less traditional, patterns less true to their Scottish roots. Tartan had come of age, its regular lines cohering with the graphic look of the future.

I remember a black-and-white tartan Pierre Cardin short coat with an exaggerated standup funnel neck, the

wide diameter of which echoed the space suit. Straight cut and slim, the coat had a bias-cut lower skirt and straight-cut top; ideas similar to Dior's but on a completely different silhouette. Shot in black and white by John French, it was ultra-modern for its time and pivotal to an era in which tartan was seen in miniskirts, playsuits, mod dresses, shorts, princess coats and capes of all lengths. Entire outfits in tartan were rare but in a *Vogue* shoot in May 1967 Twiggy was shot wearing a graphic New Look tartan playsuit, with matching tartan jacket with trimmed edges; Ronald Traeger's photo epitomised '60s style: tartan with a spark of youthful androgyny.

TARTAN GOES LUNAR

As an interlude, in 1969 a swatch of MacBean Tartan was one of the items taken to the moon by astronaut Alan Bean on *Apollo 12*, establishing tartan's truly universal status.

SUITED TO TARTAN

Tailoring was shaken up in the late 1960s too. A young man called Tommy Nutter, Savile Row-trained, was known as 'the Rebel of the Row'. He used traditional construction techniques but mixed checks and exaggerated the proportions of his suits, which were seen on Elton John, Mick Jagger and Ringo Starr. Tommy's trademark wide parallel-leg trousers were worn with elongated jackets that had exaggerated curved lapels and sleeve heads raised to the extreme. His favourite trick was to mix

checks or the same tone and colour to dramatic effect.

This wide-leg silhouette of the 1920s Oxford bag rapidly translated into the parallels and flares of the late 1960s. As '70s glam rock took over from '60s psychedelia, the likes of Noddy Holder, Rod Stewart and the Bay City Rollers were responsible for tartan's presence in the decade that taste forgot. I was a child of the '70s and my scars run deep. I can barely bring myself to write about the tartan trauma these individuals inflicted on my eyes and my ear drums. Luckily, there is an exception; beyond a shadow of a doubt, hand on my heart, the only man to wear a glam rock tartan suit with style was Marc Bolan. His more sultry approach gave his look a darkened edge (but glitter eye make-up is always a no-no).

A FETISH FOR TARTAN

It was from this period of the worst fashion mistakes in history that tartan had its own rebellion. From a small shop on London's Kings Road, Malcolm McLaren and his then-girlfriend Vivienne Westwood evolved their clothing business through teddy boy suits and rock 'n' roll, to an incredibly on-point, dramatic range of fetish wear. In 1975, tartan was about to truly rebel against all that had come before. The shop was renamed 'Seditionaries' and punk was born. With economic decline and disillusionment, there was a void to be filled with subversive ideas and tartan looked set to be reinvented for a youth culture that bristled with an anarchic energy.

PANTS

Vivienne Westwood's creation of 'bondage pants' dipped into history and her interest in fetish wear and corsets. Close-fitting tartan trousers with looped hung belted legs and zip detail became the archetypal punk look. With the addition of a short kilted apron clipped on at the waist these trousers brought together so many fetish, military and Highland elements that they've become a modern fashion icon. Recently I was asked to recreate a pair for a client in Anderson tartan, not something an established bespoke tailor would normally accept as a commission, but I did, partly to prove to myself that I could. The result felt like recreating a piece of period costume. I was using the client's measures and detailing from photographs to keep the fit and the proportions true to the original, while making them subtle enough to be worn with a velvet jacket to a black-tie dinner. It was a challenge!

Recreating a piece like this paid homage to an idea that helped spawn a youth movement. The 'Seditionaries' ranges sprang from a spell in New York where the Westwood–McLaren duo dressed the New York Dolls. This connection with one of punk's first bands was short-lived, but the subculture itself had only just germinated. Their SEX shop on the Kings Road attracted an array of diverse characters – the magnificent Viv Albertine among them – and Malcolm McLaren decided to create a punk band. You might call it 'manufactured', as the people chosen – including a young John Lydon – weren't picked for their musical ability more their attitude and outspokenness, and so the Sex Pistols were born.

The whole punk ethos was fiercely anti-establishment. Slashed garments daubed with slogans, safety pins, zips, provocation and snarling opinionated attitude were all home-made and home grown, as the youth needed a subculture to call their own. Tartan, as an outspoken cloth with a history of subversive rebellion and shade of irony to it, fitted punk's core perfectly. Tartan had become credible again, big style.

A NEW ROMANCE

The early 1980s saw the edginess of punk evolve into the high camp of the dandy-esque New Romantic look. Again, Malcolm McLaren was on the fringes, managing Adam and the Ants and Bow Wow Wow. Tartan became less relevant – though a young Adam Ant did take to the stage in a kilt – but it did fall more into the mainstream again, thanks to Laura Ashley and Ralph Lauren. Both had a romantic dream of British style. Laura Ashley with her Vaseline-lensed view that seemed to merge Jane Austen with Edwardian-era florals, and Ralph Lauren with his Anglophile designs. For me, their perspective was rose-tinted: everything was either too wealthy and affluent or too feminine and floral. Not to my taste, but I do remember Laura Ashley's below-the-knee Black Watch tartan dress with its white Peter Pan collar.

Ralph Lauren had been gaining notoriety

in the US since the mid-1970s, but it wasn't until the early 1980s that he became an inspirational brand on this side of the Atlantic. Inspired by figures such as the Duke of Windsor, he would frequently mix tartans with checks to create subtle yet distinctive looks that were very British, which he then sold back to the British. Clever!

FAR FROM COOL

At this time my fashion ideas came from the street, from music and from the American dream in the form of 'brat pack' movies. My hero was River Phoenix – and he never wore tartan. If I saw it on film it was a parody (exception: Judd Nelson's tartan shirt/denim jacket combo in *The Breakfast Club*) of the overweight salesman in a plaid sports coat, or the nerdy guy in tartan shorts. Nothing that Hollywood sold me made tartan even remotely cool.

THE IMMORTAL HIGHLANDER

All that changed when *Highlander* hit our cinema screens in 1986; a film in which Scotland and its history were again inspiring action and adventure for a new generation. The story follows an immortal Highland warrior battling with a handful of other immortals through time. Switching between the past and the present, it features Sean Connery as the Highlander's mentor and guide – and no, he wasn't wearing a kilt!

KILT CAMP

It wasn't until 1987 when I sat up and noticed that there was a glimmer of cool left in tartan, and that this came from Paris in the form of Jean Paul Gaultier. It seemed like the Auld Alliance had returned with this peroxide blond Breton-striped kilted *enfant terrible* of Parisian couture. He took the essence of punk and the craft of the kilt and celebrated them into a sexy Eurotrash catwalk carnival of high theatrical style. Still not quite my thing, but there was hope! Gaultier even crowbarred in elements of power-dressing, with the acid-yellow-and-black tartan he created for his tailoring. This exuberant mash-up of capitalism and rebellion made the collection jar, for me at least, with its own internal conflict, but it was easy to consume and put Gaultier on the fashion map.

Jean Paul Gaultier's distinctive look often features a kilt, but with black biker boots and a Breton-striped long-sleeved T; he liberates the kilt from formality and conventional masculinity into a celebratory, peacock aesthetic. His genius is in freedom and expressiveness, drawing inspiration from history, from global cultures and playing with traditional gender roles. 'You either design clothes for the woman you want, or the woman you want to be' has to be my favourite John Paul Gaultier quote.

QUEEN VIVIENNE

The late 1980s and early 1990s saw Vivienne Westwood reintroduce strong notions of tartan into her collections; in an extraordinary mix-up of ideas from

Scotland, Texas, punk and the Village People she created the Tartan Cowboy. Always drawing from history and then the British aristocracy, tartan was a constant. Her AW90 collection 'Portrait' gave sleek silhouettes, with defined tailoring on the female form, using Royal Stewart and Dress Stewart tartans. The AW91 'Dressing Up' collection focused on the masquerade of Lord Murray and Lord Tullibardine, bestowing a theatrical edge or exaggerated lines to the tartan. AW93's 'Anglomania' took the theatre of tartan a step further to use silk taffeta in a full-skirted tartan dress; layered, ruched, full of period opulence. Vivienne Westwood remains one of tartan's biggest advocates; she has created cloths with Lochcarron that include McBrick, inspired by the London cityscape.

TARTAN GOES GRUNGE

But it wasn't until a band from Aberdeen – no, the one near Seattle – had a 1991 hit with 'Smells Like Teen Spirit' that music culture made tartan accessible again to the (youthful) masses.

Maybe this sounds a little unlikely, so please bear with me: the tartan link isn't as weak as you might think. Nirvana were at the forefront of 'grunge' and their music was spawned from punk, metal and indie rock, with themes of social alienation, neglect, betrayal and emotional isolation. It didn't float my boat at that time. I was more of a 'skate betty', but the grunge and skate scenes have their crossover points . . . and so, back to tartan. Part of the grunge uniform was the tartan or plaid shirt, worn open over a faded T-shirt and washed-out ripped jeans; mid-length surfer hair with stubble (for the boys) completed the look. 'Did Kurt Cobain ever wear a kilt?' I hear you ask. No, but he did wear a prim, buttoned-up floral dress on the cover of *The Face* in September 1993.

This is the point where tartan had its first relevance in my fashion world. It was glimmering on my horizon with brands like Palace, Silas, APC, YMC, Volcom, Emerica, Dickies, Carhartt and Stussy. The tartan check shirt was a definite grunge crossover, and skaters had adopted workwear brands for their lack of fashion edge, their relative cheapness and their durability. Oh, how times change! I sound more like a mum than a creative saying that, but it's true.

Fashion is circular, sure, but for me the essence of youth culture is in how it refuses to follow the expected or mainstream route, but is energised by its own creativity to define its set . . . or clan? Back in the mid-1990s this was still the case, but now youthful reliance on social media as the place in which to discover trends leads them away from individuality and towards mass-market conformity. (There I go, being a mum again!) But a deeper delve into the realms of social media highlights breathtakingly imaginative creative pioneers. We need to support and nurture the unconventional, to celebrate our global cultural diversity.

TARTAN HEROICS AND ANTI-HEROES

And in the mid-1990s tartan was given swashbuckling filmic life as Mel Gibson and Liam Neeson portrayed iconic Scottish heroes, William Wallace and Rob Roy. Hollywood epics that championed the Scottish underdog against the might of the English Crown, and tartan was most certainly worn. But should it have been? In centuries to come, will these films be viewed as historical fact? Like the medieval monks writing the stories of King Arthur over six hundred years after he lived, can we take these films as in any way accurate? True or otherwise, they entertained and wowed. They promoted the romance of Scottish legends to a worldwide audience and sparked international interest in Scotland once more. Perhaps, to a lesser degree, they gave pride back to a nation: three years later, the 1998 vote for devolution was an overwhelming 'Yes'.

Then again in 1996 Danny Boyle and Irvine Welsh painted a much grittier Scotland in *Trainspotting*, a film that crackles with the harshness of an imagined Scottish dystopia. No tartan here except in parody; the film could be seen as a pastiche of *Whisky Galore!* (*Heroin Galore!*, more like), dealing as it did with substance abuse, male isolation and petty criminality.

Designer Paul Smith entered the 1990s era of national pride with his 'True Brit' collections. The general mood in the UK echoed that of the 1960s: hemlines were rising, trousers were narrowing, and there was optimism about the economic future. The patterns used in the True Brit collections were enlarged or obscured tartans to give a larger sett and simplified

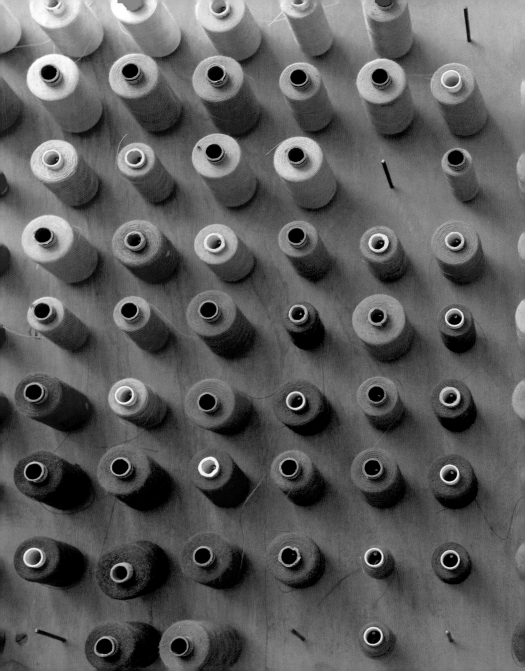

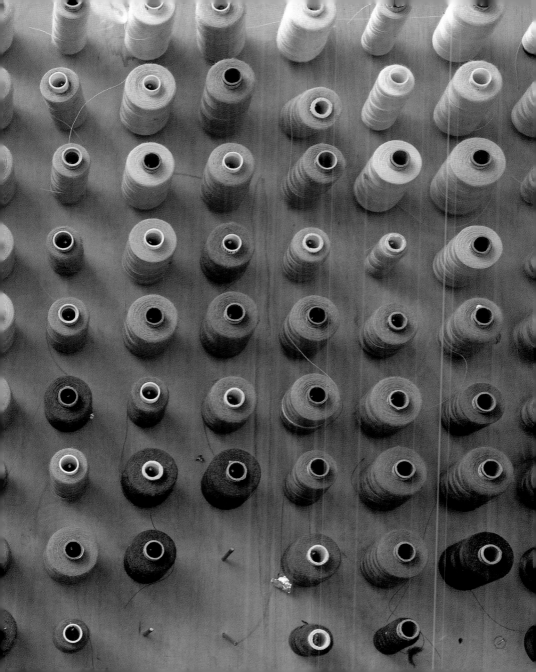

pattern. They were striking yet minimal; plain suits were accented with tartan shirts, but they were tailored and made from finer cottons, not workwear but more city wear, sharp and edgy.

TARTAN ARTISTRY

At this time the 'Highland Rape' collection from Alexander McQueen was unveiled. AW95 showcased the collection which was to establish McQueen not only as a world-class designer, but as an activist driven by the pride of a nation. The title was not as explicit as the press would like you to believe. It relates to the English rape of the Scottish throne, along with the horror of the Highland Clearances. These powerful looks and his thought-provoking fashion philosophy gave McQueen the status more of an artist than a designer. He saw far beyond the shortbread tin, and relayed the dreich and ruthless nature of his heritage, telling of dramatic turbulence between two nations.

'Highland Rape' used tartan sparingly; McQueen conveyed his message with paper-thin layered dyed silks, portraying a worn-down and weathered look of garments and characters who were mere ghosts of their former selves. It wasn't until 2006 with 'Widows of Culloden' that McQueen re-imagined his Scottish roots with more romance and poetry; this time to accompany his theme of the widows after the 1746 Jacobite defeat. The outfits were inspired by tradition; elaborate ruffs, slighted petticoats, and theatrical evening attire was the basis for the collection. The feminine form focused more around the waist: heavily bodiced and bustled. McQueen tartan was accented with ornate brocades, rich black velvet and messed black lace. The whole feeling was a gothic, opulent and elaborate view of classical and baronial Scotland.

Between these two collections Scotland as a nation regained its pride, a little of its identity and certainly its passion for independence. With a new millennium looming, there was optimism and uncertainty, and the population homed in on things which were steadfast and familiar, tartan among them.

TARTAN FOR THE MILLENNIUM

In AW2005 the world's catwalks were once again alight with the colours and vibrancy of tartan. Paul Smith focused on more muted tonal checks for skirts, trousers and jackets, while Burberry had been re-imagined under the watchful creative direction of Christopher Bailey. I, like many others, saw the Burberry tartan as a lining fabric for raincoats, then all of a sudden there was an international explosion of check.

THE BURBERRY BRAND

From a single shop in Basingstoke in 1856, Thomas Burberry proved that if you can do one thing supremely well you will win renown for it. Worn by gentry, his functional outerwear went to the South Pole with Shackleton, was recognised by the War Office and became the 'trench' coat used by officers in the Great War. The instantly recognisable Burberry check was introduced in 1924, and I am still unsure if it is truly classed as a tartan.

By the 21st century, the task was to transform a very functional, masculine brand into something aspirational: not just for dull days and wet British weather (and a smattering of football 'casuals'), but a look of elegance and femininity which could be worn the world over. With the careful design of Rose Marie Bravo and the figure of Kate Moss, Burberry adopted a covetable, international persona. From bikinis to handbags, fragrances to scarves the brand's 'Prorsum' collection reclaimed its luxury identity.

A TARTAN TAKEOVER

Over the past decade, the cloth has been used cautiously and sparingly by fashion houses the world over. Never quite in fashion and never quite out of fashion, it always has a presence in collections from Westwood to Balenciaga. Its unmistakeable form has been muted, abstracted, enlarged, weathered, monochromed or miniaturised, but is still recognisable and still quintessentially Scottish; sometimes it's even noted by its absence from genuinely Scottish films.

Even so, it would appear that AW2019 marked the season of the 'tartan takeover' with designers including Christian Dior, Marine Serre, Lanvin, Unravel and Rokh using tartan checks for their key pieces. The patterns were as varied as they were

colourful, from 'buffalo check' (Rob Roy tartan) to complex Glen checks. The standout piece for me was from Maria Grazia Chiuri for Dior: a deep green and ink variant of the Rob Roy tartan used in a simple chore jacket with piped edges. It was her realignment of the feminine image which attracted me; there is female form but at the same time a relaxed sense of function. She references 1950s teddy-girl influences and strong bold patterns to give presence and appeal.

Marine Serre has twisted her tartans into complex forms and silhouettes; there are hourglass-shaped coats of tartan, and a long caped poncho offset with masks of tartan over the models' faces. The Rokh fall collection provides a different look with deconstructed belted coats, matched with loose-fitting trousers, along with skirt and turtleneck outfits. Ben Taverniti for Unravel combines tartans and flannels; looks include tartan trews with denim backs, along with trench coats combined with moto jackets. Then Bruno Sialelli's debut for Lanvin provides us with tartan on cosy knits, capes, outwear and even some kilts!

AFTER A FASHION

It might seem that through all the eras of fashion, tartan has stayed the same, but the way people see it and use it is constantly changing. Surely proof that it is a truly timeless cloth with a broad and far-reaching appeal. But however and wherever tartan is used, the history and heritage remain: slightly functional, slightly vibrant, slightly poetic and slightly theatrical . . . tartan transcends gender, location, age, class and climate. What other fabric can make such a claim? My guess is not even denim – and I doubt there are any mills still weaving in Nîmes.

THE STORY OF A COMMISSION

It's easy to look back and talk about other people's creations, but when I was asked to create a one-off couture outfit for a global pageant, I had an inkling how those tailors of 1745 must have felt. And I certainly knew that if you are presented with a brief to encompass the 'Spirit of Scotland', first off, you do not choose the Spirit of Scotland tartan. My commission was for a pageant

in Thailand, a global event, televised live. To call it 'Miss World' is to do it injustice; it was as much a celebration of style and beauty as intelligence and grace.

The young woman who approached me was Abigail Gliksten and I was anxious for both her and myself when I heard what the project entailed. There was no doubt in my mind that tartan had to be the cloth. Tweed would be too muted. We needed to be theatrical, elegant, sassy and well tailored – that way we would hopefully take the 'tarty' out of tartan.

Our choice of cloth – the Isle of Skye tartan – turned out to be surprisingly easy. Abigail's family hails from that area of Scotland, making it a natural choice. Her

fair hair and complexion needed something feminine yet bold, and it was a perfect fit. The colours were neither too masculine nor too muted; a combination of heather and moss best describes it.

INSPIRATIONAL ISLE

Although I have talked about district tartans as a thing from the past, this one was only recently designed and commissioned. The cloth was instigated by Mrs Rosemary Nicolson Samios, an Australian of Skye descent. It was designed as part of a global competition, which, ironically, was won by a weaver, Angus MacLeod, from the Isle of Lewis. The Isle of Skye tartan was first woven in commercial quantities in 1993, so in the lifetime of tartan it is a new kid on the block.

The colours pay faithful homage to the tones of the Isle of Skye, with strong heathery purples, subtle burgundy brown and fresh sea greens with a pale grey fine stripe running through. Its design gives a contemporary twist to traditional ideas, and moves away from the harsher, more direct colours of the past to a tastefully muted and considered palette. This beautiful cloth was famously worn by Her Majesty the Queen at the opening of the Scottish Parliament in 2004, which must count as the royal seal of approval.

With the cloth decided, back to Abigail. Her slender figure needed presence and so, with clever use of the sett and taking inspiration from Dior's early shapes, I designed a full-length tartan dress coat with contrast cuff and collar detail. The bodice of the coat was sharply tailored to her figure and the full-length skirt section was broad cut on the bias to give more fluid movement when she walked. The front facing from the hem was shaped upwards echoing the idea of a Victorian riding coat; the collar and cuffs were finished in a golden Harris Tweed. I felt the urge to bring the two cloths together to tell a tasteful tale.

Underneath the dress coat, I designed a boned tartan bustier and a pair of tailored shorts – not hot pants, but as a nod to Twiggy and a 1960s twist. To complete the outfit, Sally-Ann Provan, an incredible Edinburgh-based milliner, created a felted wool button-shaped fascinator with an eye-catching plume of pheasant feathers.

NOT QUITE A NATIONAL COSTUME

There was an air of intelligence, feminine strength and patriotism, with Abigail's grace, vitality and personality complementing the look. It was a departure from anything I had tailored before; my idea was to create a national costume, but without being too obvious (or kilted!). The intention was regal, harking back to a bygone age of formality but with contemporary hints to enhance Abigail's natural beauty as a modern young woman. The joy with which Abigail *owned* this outfit on stage made me incredibly proud; an unexpected commission well received; my mission accomplished.

A MOST EXCELLENT ARCHIVIST

One woman I have met since creating Abigail's outfit would have been a great source of knowledge when I was researching early ladies' Highland dress. She has perhaps seen more vintage and antique cloth and clothing in her studies and her career than anyone could ever hope to, and I am slightly jealous. Dr Rosie Waine specialises in contextual costume: looking at and understanding the correctness of dress from each age would perhaps be an easier way to describe her work. It's a job that seems driven by a genuine passion – an obsession even?

One of Dr Waine's recent projects was curating the 2019 *Wild and Majestic* exhibition at the National Museum of Scotland. Her precision and attention to detail make this remarkable exhibition a joy to view. It has a sense of purity to it, not at all overdressed. I've learned that Dr Waine prefers not to 'mix' her eras, so I guess my creation for Abigail might not be exactly her cup of tea. But it's evident she likes to keep her clear-eyed professional focus for the cloths of the past on that which is true and honest. So much of Scottish history is embellished – you might even say fabricated – that aiming for a simple clarity is, for me, a refreshing mantra to have.

Q&A: ROSIE WAINE
Textile researcher and curator

Vixy Rae: When did the idea for the Wild and Majestic exhibition come from?

Rosie Waine: I joined the curatorial team working on *Wild and Majestic: Romantic Visions of Scotland* (National Museum of Scotland: 26 June to 10 November 2019) in 2018. As a textile and dress historian, it was my job to explore the role played by fashion in the era of Scottish Romanticism and to select the most appropriate examples from the museum collection. Naturally, tartan and Highland dress were central to telling that tale.

Did you have a firm idea of the items you wanted or were there some surprise offerings from private collections?

Devising the costume and textile displays

for *Wild and Majestic* was a true labour of love. I wanted to show the full range of engagement with tartan across the 18th and 19th centuries, while still communicating what the fabric symbolises for people around the world today. In the years that spanned the Battle of Culloden and the building of Balmoral, tartan was transformed into a badge of identity that resonated both within and outwith Scotland. I think that still holds true.

The 'romantic' allure of tartan is obvious, but its true history is frequently obscured by the mythology that tends to creep up around it – clan tartans being a prime example. With that in mind, I chose to feature garments that would demonstrate the commercial or everyday side of tartan. In addition, I wanted to show that it wasn't a purely masculine fabric reserved for use in the tailored suits of Highland dress worn by the country's elites. By curating displays of women's and children's wear, I wanted to communicate what an adaptable, attractive commodity tartan had become by the turn of the 19th century.

It's interesting how historical events inspire poetry and art, and now these creative offerings seem to support the history. Would you agree?
One of the things that quickly becomes apparent when you dig into the art and literature of the Romantic era is how much of it has a basis in reality. The sensationalist or sentimental nature of the material can blind people to the fact that those who

created Romantic works were often taking their inspiration from life, history, from the physical world around them. It was never a matter of pure invention.

An excellent example can be found in Sir Walter Scott's novel *Rob Roy*, which contains a scene in which the hero explains how his sporran is booby-trapped with a set of pistols, primed to go off should someone tamper with the cantle. Scott took inspiration for this scene from a weaponised sporran cantle made during the 18th century that belonged to the Society of Antiquaries of Scotland, an object that still exists and that features in *Wild and Majestic*. It's an episode that neatly exemplifies that blend of romance and reality, this use of a real object to inform a work of historical fiction.

Much of Scotland's history has been embellished over the ages. Do you have a favourite true story from the exhibition which is stranger than fiction?
The Romantic era is full of peculiar stories and larger-than-life characters. We tried to profile as many of these in the exhibition as we could.

One of the more contradictory figures is Alasdair Ranaldson Macdonell of Glengarry, 15th Chief of Glengarry. He was quite a dandy and wore the most fashionable cuts of Highland dress. Though he famously championed the romanticised Highland ideal in his day-to-day life at Invergarry and during his visits to the social hubs of Edinburgh and London, he also took steps

SIR WALTER SCOTT, RECREATED BY STEWART CHRISTIE

to clear tenants off his land to make way for the coming of the sheep.

If I had to pick a favourite story it would be Queen Victoria's boat ride on Loch Tay in September 1842. A child of the Romantic movement and an avid reader of Sir Walter Scott, when she visited Scotland for the first time she was swept up by the pageantry performed by her Highland hosts. On this boat ride, she was serenaded by a piper and a chorus of Gaelic song as they proceeded down the loch. She was introduced to one of the oarsmen, John MacDougall of Dunollie, after she noticed the historic Brooch of Lorn pinned to his breast. He informed her that it had been captured by one of his ancestors from Robert the Bruce in 1306. Looking at the brooch today, you can still see fragments of the MacDougall tartan caught in the setting around the charm stone.

How many tartan garments does the National Museum hold in its archive? Do many hold makers' labels?
National Museums Scotland holds a small but significant collection of Highland dress and tartan clothing, ranging in date from the early 18th to the late 20th century. The collection is particularly rich in material from the early 19th century, a time when tartan was emerging as a popular fashion fabric in Britain and when Highland dress was becoming known as the national costume of Scotland.

FLORA MACDONALD, RECREATED BY STEWART CHRISTIE

At the end of the 18th century, Highland dress was undergoing a transformation driven by fashionable taste. Highland elites brought what had been a predominantly rural form of traditional dress, associated with the warrior culture of Gaelic society, in line with dominant male clothing styles in Europe. This period of sartorial experimentation is well represented in the collection. The earliest Highland dress suits held show off a variety of tailoring styles, which document – among other things – the development of the modern kilt, as well as the rise of clan tartans.

Some objects in the collection do hold makers' labels, including garments by the Highland dress outfitters Kinloch Anderson and fabric samples by the influential tartan-weaving company, Wilsons of Bannockburn.

Out of all these pieces – not including John Brown's tartan underpants! – which is your favourite piece?
One of my favourite outfits is a suit of fine hard tartan faced with green silk, purchased in Edinburgh by an English Jacobite called Sir John Hynde Cotton when he visited the city in 1744. Just three years prior, Bonnie Prince Charlie had appeared in full Highland dress at an Easter festival in Rome, a publicity stunt meant to demonstrate his family's historic links with Scotland and – by extension – their claims to the British throne.

MARY QUEEN OF SCOTS, RECREATED BY STEWART CHRISTIE

Cotton was clearly impressed by this patriotic use of Highland dress by the exiled prince. Evidently a large man, Cotton's jacket, trews and plaid are quite imposing when seen together on a mannequin. He would have cut an impressive figure wearing this vivid tartan suit in support of the exiled House of Stuart, especially if sporting it in his home county of Cambridgeshire!

Tartan outfits from this period are rare, because in the aftermath of the last Jacobite rising of 1745–46, the wearing of Highland dress in Scotland was banned by Act of Parliament. I think one of the reasons that Cotton's suit survived intact is because it was owned and worn by an Englishman, not a Scot.

It would appear every aspect of tartan and its history has been garnished with romance. Is it hard to determine fact from fiction when presented with so much information?

Romance is part of tartan's history, and it cannot be ignored. Trying to figure out how and when that romanticism emerged has always fascinated me. I've found the trick is to approach everything with a critical eye and to not project too many personal feelings. It's good to keep a certain measure of distance, as it's so easy to get pulled along in the glamour that tartan evokes.

Researching the fabric is very different from wearing it, however, and I'd never want to diminish anyone's sense of pride

ROBERT BURNS, RECREATED BY STEWART CHRISTIE

in a thing that they love. All I ever want to do is tell someone something that they might not have known before, so that they can love tartan for all its many, often contradictory, histories.

The female aspect of tartan is often less well noted. Were there any heroines of the Jacobite uprisings besides Flora MacDonald?
How Flora MacDonald emerged as the poster girl for female Jacobites is an interesting twist in the tale of tartan. The fabric played a significant part in her rise to stardom.

When MacDonald was released from the Tower of London in 1747, she commissioned a portrait of herself from Richard Wilson, who depicted her wearing a fabulous chequered gown of red and black, embellished with white ribbons. Not long after that, the celebrated Scottish artist Allan Ramsay painted her wrapped in a tartan plaid, with white roses in her hair. This trend was quickly picked up and widely circulated by British printmakers, leading people to hang cheap engravings of Ramsay's image in their own homes.

As some regarded the cause of the exiled House of Stuart as a national one, the aim of images showing MacDonald swathed in rebel tartan was to mark her actions out as brave and patriotic. That MacDonald was pressured by her family into helping the Prince and that she had no true stake in the Jacobites' fight is a fact often lost in the retelling. That the striking visual of her dressed in tartan still dominates her story is testament to the symbolic power of the fabric, and how it has continued to resonate down through the centuries to the present day.

We have the notion that women were lovelorn bystanders smitten by Bonnie Prince Charlie's romantic image. But was female input to the Jacobite cause more involved?

This is something that pops up again and again, and it's a perception that dates right back to the 1745–46 Rising itself. Those who supported the Hanoverian dynasty liked to paint Jacobite women as foolish and lustful, with an unnatural attraction to this mysterious young man from 'over the water'. It was a means of explaining away the actions of women working against the status quo. In reality, the majority of women who supported the House of Stuart did what they did because they believed in the cause.

Do you think it is time for an exhibition highlighting the achievements of Scotland's women?

Absolutely! The role of women in creating history is often overlooked or underplayed. Take the history of tartan, which is dominated by the masculine silhouette cut by Highland dress. People seldom think of the women who helped to rehabilitate tartan in the 18th century, transforming it from rebel fabric to national symbol.

Jean Maxwell, the Duchess of Gordon, for example, was just such a woman. At the same time as tartan was becoming inextricably linked to the Highland military through its use by Scottish soldiers serving at home and abroad, she was introducing tartan to the royal court – bringing it right to the heart of cultural and political power in Britain.

WILLIAM WALLACE, RECREATED BY STEWART CHRISTIE

TAM O'SHANTER, RECREATED BY STEWART CHRISTIE

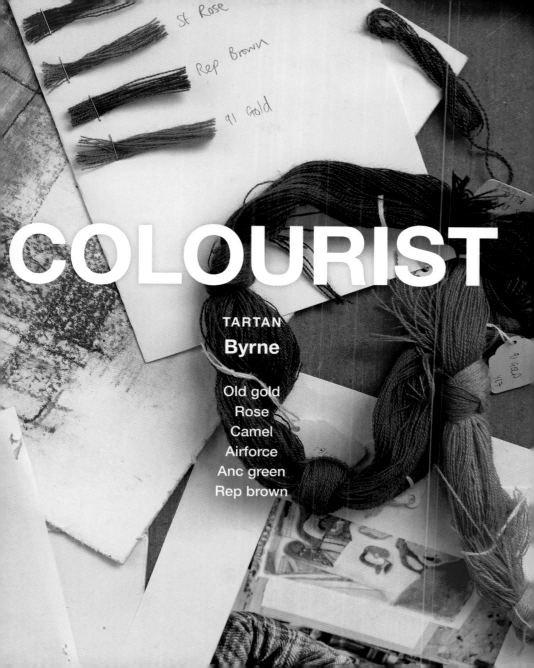

COLOURIST

TARTAN
Byrne

Old gold
Rose
Camel
Airforce
Anc green
Rep brown

THE HUMAN USE OF COLOUR

My whole life has been affected by colour. My friends all know my deep love of rainbows and how such a simple thing brings me an inner sense of joy and happiness. But before you start to think I am a new-age, born-again hippy, I better explain myself. I like to plait my hair, and I care passionately about the environment, but I'm absolutely not a hippy (not on the outside anyway). And nor is my home decorated with an abundance of rainbow motifs or themed in a polychromatic, haphazard way. My colourist tendencies are more monolithic, veering towards the dictatorial. Which means some might say I am something of an authoritarian colourist.

In Scotland, nature provides a world of colour with the changing seasons, and even in the centre of Edinburgh seasonal changes are felt by shifts in colour in the city. The architecture is stunning and the topography unique, but I believe the colours of Edinburgh are what makes it one of the most picturesque cities in the world. This is what inspires me. But where my authoritarian colourist tendencies shine are with the human use of colour in all its guises. This simply means that certain colour choices work for me and others really don't; they just make me feel 'hate'.

I have been aware of and influenced by fashion and design all my adult life, but as a child my Steiner education opened my mind to the use of colour and its effects on people, the whole way in which we view the world around us. In its simplest forms, nature provides the basis and backdrop for our feelings and emotions when it comes to colour. Red will make our heart beat faster, whereas green will calm the soul.

My own personal notions of colour,

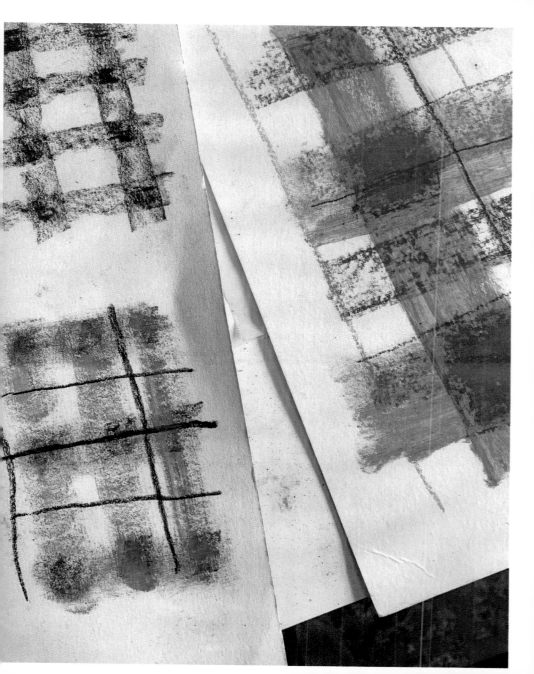

ingrained in my psyche, have always somehow resisted the structure and colour of tartan. I recognise it as more of a mathematical and masculine composition, rather than soft and melange. Tartan's strong tones and defined contrasts have fallen in and out of favour over the centuries, but changes in weaving and dyeing have affected its look over time too.

TARTAN IN COLOUR

It occurs to me that – with changes in fashion, style and colour, and also the straightforward impact of personal taste from one generation to the next – tartan must naturally evolve in order to survive and to connect with its wearers. No one would expect, or want, a fabric with such cultural resonance and historical reach to stay the same, or it would just remain the cloth of the past, something to be looked at in museums or worn purely as costume.

And this is surely one of the pivotal reasons why there are so many variants – not all of them subtle – in the named family and clan tartans. The numerous variants in existence today are also thanks to the commercial imperative which, simply put, holds that if there is more choice there is more potential for sales.

You might think it is the pattern of tartan which changes, but in actual fact it is the colour. Changes in colour can dramatically change the look of the cloth and make it seem as if it's a different pattern. The impact of colour combinations is tremendous. We've all seen those family tartans that are truly retina burning; bold choices, which certainly turn heads, but not always for the right reasons.

Each tartan is designed by its 'sett', the thread count which denotes the pattern. So the pattern remains constant – it's just the colours and the shading that change.

VARIOUS VARIANTS

Today we have six types of named variant: Modern, Ancient, Muted, Hunting, Weathered and Dress.

It is worth mentioning that each tartan's named variant bears no relation to when the cloth was actually woven or to the type of dye used on the yarn. Some consumers assume that 'Ancient' means it comes from a roll of cloth or a type of yarn from the past. I'm sorry to say that's just not true. Likewise, it's not the case that the yarn for the cloth will be dyed using ancient dyes; again, it's just a name, and I will explain why.

THE SAME THREAD PALETTE CAN BE USED ON ANY NUMBER OF
SETTS TO CREATE COMPLETELY DIFFERENT DESIGNS.

THE DIFFERENCE IN DYES

With the development of chemical dyes, which took over from natural dyes from the 1850s onwards, the intensity, tone and vibrancy of tartan's colours have undergone significant change. In the past, natural vegetable dyes were used to dye yarn in every colour and shade. These gave the early tartans a rich, deep colour, but the beauty of natural dyes was no match for the cost efficiency and predictability of chemical dyes, which also offered more with regards to continuity. And so, in nearly all cases, the natural was quickly overtaken by the chemical and the visual aesthetic of tartan changed accordingly.

Historically William Wilson & Sons – a mill that is sadly no longer around – produced generations of colours from natural dyes. Their skills have stood the test of time when it comes to how the colours have lasted and aged.

In the archive at Stewart Christie & Co.

there are two pattern books which were completed in 1885. These hold fabrics created with a combination of chemical and vegetable dyes. While there is certainly a difference between these and the tartans of today, looking back it is sometimes hard to tell natural from chemical. But the keen eye will soon see there are subtle differences and patterns in how the yarns have taken the dyes. It's not that the sett has become obscured, more that the texture and the depth of colour are acutely different.

These variants offer a useful explanation of why the colour of the cloth is the way it is. In most cases there is a degree of romantic licence. But whether these variants are built on myth or on truth, on mystery or on credibility, they all add up to the majesty of the cloth.

VARIANT: ANCIENT
Sometimes called Old or Vegetable Colours

The cloths in these pattern books echo the colours supposedly created in the past from natural dyes. In the 1930s these tones became popular, possibly as a backlash against the darker shades from the earlier Victorian period. This was a period between the First and Second World Wars where the prosperity of the time was reflected in the way people dressed. The tones of natural dyes are much lighter and brighter; they are fresher and feel better suited to wearing in the day than in the evening.

Everything moves in cycles, so the creation of these ancient palettes might have been due to the ageing of the natural or the early chemical dyes. For example, a kilt owned by one's great grandfather may have been originally woven in what we might class as modern colours. The said kilt, having been worn by previous generations and 'handed down', then may have become bleached by years of daylight.

Early dyes did react differently to modern dyes with prolonged wear in bright sunlight. This would result in a much lighter overall tone. This would have happened slowly, and so it would perhaps have been assumed that this was an ancient colour. Nostalgia, like sex, sells and in the case of tartan, it's a nostalgia that has been romanced by the passage of time. Those old, muted colours that give rise to feelings of nostalgia for one generation might simply be old hat for the next.

VARIANT: WEATHERED
Sometimes called Reproduction

This variant is not yet classed as a strictly true and pure variant by those in the know. Rather, it is a modern reincarnation of the idea of a 'true' Ancient cloth. It is how we might envisage a cloth from the times of the Jacobite uprisings, with yarn dyed using natural dyes and colourways that would reflect the land, giving more tweed-like and earthy hues.

Again, there is a story here, and it's a story that is more romantic myth than fact. In 1946 an archaeological dig on the battlefield of Culloden unearthed a swatch of tartan – and it's from there that the idea came. The

cloth had been buried in the peat for over 200 years. For two centuries, its colours had absorbed the colour of the peat, become muted and almost over-dyed by it.

This is by far my favourite variant and story. We have a tartan romantically absorbing the colour of the land, buried deep and hidden from history. It has also become the closest variant to tweed that exists, and possibly to the really true early tartans too. This variant has been faithfully re-created by the DC Dalgliesh Mill, in Selkirk. It was developed to fulfil a gap in the market to satisfy an earthier and more camouflaged tartan, one which translated well into streetwear and offered an altogether more austere version of the cloth. It also has a strong appeal to those who had been scarred by the garish tartan of the 1980s and wanted to discover variant with a more authentic, softer feel . . . And yes, I have fitted capri pants and a waistcoat in this one!

VARIANT: MODERN
Sometimes called Ordinary

It's clear to anyone that calling the cloth 'ordinary' wasn't really going to sell it. Instead, we say 'modern', but this variant really signifies the point in history where dyes changed from natural to chemical. In 1856, Perkin's purple was the first chemical colour created and this was a complete mistake. Chemistry student William Perkin had been set a challenge by his professor to synthesise quinine. In one attempt the oxidisation process created a black solid, which signified another failure.

But, as mentioned in the Dyeing chapter, when he cleaned out the flask, Perkin noticed the chemical reaction created a wonderful purple colour. This was dubbed 'mauveine'. By the end of the decade mauveine was extremely fashionable and came to be one of the defining colours of the Victorian era. And so, the unintended consequence of a chemistry experiment spurred on a whole industry.

But the colours created were much stronger and more intense; they lacked the harmonious subtlety of the natural dyes. These darker colours fitted the mood of the time. Sombre and powerful, they were quickly adopted by the military, and it was this same approach that made the shading of the government tartan almost black.

The darkness of the modern colours is taken from navy, green and black. In combination, these give rise to a cloth more suited for modern evening wear; certainly, it has a formal, less playful appearance. It seems counter-intuitive, but depending on your perspective, the modern variant is in fact older than some of the ancient ones: many of the ancient colours were created in the years before the Second World War.

VARIANT: MUTED
Sometimes called Antique

The world of fashion likes to reinvent itself every season, but tartan usually works its transitions into the changing of the generations, so it moves a little slower. This variant was a fairly recent development hailing from the early 1970s . . . often seen as the decade that taste forgot.

These shades were a commercial undertaking and the best way to describe them is as representing a point between the ancient and the modern colours, making the ancient more wearable and the modern less wearable (at least to my mind). They are how – after the mini-revival in 1960s fashion – the tartan industry chose to show that it was keeping up with the times and reinventing itself for a new market.

From a colourist and purist perspective, this variant is characterised by less balancing of the shades, which gives it a slightly gaudy look. But this, of course, was entirely consistent with the fashions of the time.

VARIANT: HUNTING
Never called sporting, but perhaps it should be!

You might think, with all the romance and folklore surrounding these variants, that the Highlanders would have a special tartan for hunting in, but again all is myth. The terminology simply reflects the use of more greens and blues as the tartan's primary colours.

This is all very well, unless your clan tartan happens to have a lot of green and blue already in it. Thus, certain clans do not have a Hunting variant, so the moniker 'hunting' relates to the toning of the tartan rather than the usage of it. The further you investigate, the clearer it becomes that the line between truth and fiction is constantly blurred and that this blurring is specifically used to commercial advantage. In some respects, this holds true of Sir Walter Scott's role in the multifaceted life of tartan.

VARIANT: DRESS

This variant has to be my least favourite. If I were Queen of Tartan, I would decree that it should only be worn if you are a nine-year-old child as part of a Highland dance uniform. No exceptions. To articulate dress tartan in its simplest form, it's created by taking a perfectly nice tartan and replacing its main colour with white – and BOOM! What you have is a tartan best suited to the very young and to those who are the epitome of ironic chic. Perhaps this is a little bit harsh, so for the sake of tartan impartiality, I will elaborate.

The inspiration for this variant does have a real historical basis; it hails from women's traditional wear of the eighteenth century. The fashion was for ladies to wear a large, draped wrap called an 'earasaid', made from white- or cream-based tartan

(with the exception of the dress MacLeod which has yellow instead of white; a look popular in the 1980s). This suggests that 'dress' is a variant that should perhaps only be worn by women, and I have to admit I agree!

Another name for Dress is Dancers' Tartan. Whenever I hear this I can't help but smile: in Scottish slang 'ya dancer!' means something is excellent or brilliant.

AN ARTIST'S TARTAN

With my love of colour I thought I should seek a second opinion on tartan from someone who has spent his whole life surrounded by colour and has an eye for it quite unlike any other. And with that in mind, I was absolutely honoured to chat to the renowned Scottish artist and playwright, Mr John Byrne. John has designed everything from carpets to Penguin book jackets, album covers to stage sets, and so I took the chance to ask him about his art and his ideas on tartan.

THE BYRNE PROJECT

It was such a pleasure creating a tartan with one of the most stylish and artistic men in Scotland. John, like myself, struggles with some of the more tacky and obvious elements of tartan and its uses.

We giggled about this connection and he was very happy to experiment with pastel and paper to find more subtle, natural tones as he imagined them on the loom.

Working with a true colourist and man of such good taste seemed like one of the most fun ways of developing a new tartan. The mill were delighted with our collaboration and will feature it in their fashion mood boards alongside the likes of Stewart Christie, Vivienne Westwood and Chanel, creating a real hall of tartan design fame.

Q&A: JOHN BYRNE
Playwright and artist
Vixy Rae: Is tartan something you have embraced or avoided in your life?
John Byrne: Since I come from a lengthy Irish background, tartan hasn't figured much in my family. My forebears were McShanes, Byrnes and Largies.

Do you have many tartan garments in your current wardrobe?
I have a few tartan items in my wardrobe – for example, a tartan scarf, a tartan-esque lumber jacket, and I used to have a rather nice kilt which I found in a charity shop, but which I never wore.

Are the colours in your tartan palette symbolic or artistic?
Artistic.

Do you feel tartan is now a pastiche and a parody, or does it still represent a credible and historic notion of Scotland?
A bit of both, I'd say. When I hear the pipes and drums and watch the Scottish regiments on parade I do get a lump in my throat and a tear in my eye.

I found your tartan ideas a quite beautiful use of colour. What do you think of Lochcarron's translation of those ideas?
I absolutely love Lochcarron's interpretation of my rather inept rendering of my sketches!

STYLES

TARTAN
Buchanan

Rep yellow
Rep red
Rep green
Rep white
Rep blue

A BOY CALLED LEE

The bloodied history and faux romance of Scotland has inspired so many. Most notable, prolific and boundary-pushing of these, in my own narratives of fashion, is that of an East End boy called Lee, known to the world as Alexander McQueen. Lee's Scottish grandmother introduced him to his genealogy – McQueen's father was from Skye; after McQueen's untimely death in 2010, his ashes were scattered at Kilmuir on the remote western coast of Skye.

For Lee, as a young man with a fierce passion for clothing, this personal heritage inspired a collection which challenged and repulsed. His breakthrough collection provoked with the uncomfortable title of 'Highland Rape' and, in March 1995, its brilliance cast Alexander McQueen as the *enfant terrible* of high fashion.

HIGHLAND RAPE

Many consider Highland Rape to be the moment when McQueen staked his claim as a world-class designer. The show, McQueen's sixth collection, was staged in the British Fashion Council Marquee outside the Natural History Museum in London. The catwalk was scattered with heather, but that's where the romance ended. A soundtrack of dance music with the heavy discord of tolling church bells

was the collection's sonic backdrop. Even the show's invitation caused controversy. The image on the front was of a surgical wound stitched with a suturing needle.

The MacQueen tartan – a clan tartan, not Alexander McQueen's own creation – is a dramatic blood-red-and-black sett with the startling addition of golden yellow. McQueen showcased it extensively in his Highland Rape pieces; my sense is that his deeply personal attachment to his family's heritage marked a self-reflective journey for the young designer. However, the representation of 'Scottishness' was not simply a creative device in this instance. In McQueen's hands, it was a visceral reaction against romantic mythology; his work gave voice to a graphic and violent historical narrative.

My interpretation is that McQueen's passion – and rage – was ignited by his knowledge of the Highland Clearances and the warring with the English. He was vehement that these struggles were not to be reduced (to quote his words) – 'to fucking haggis, fucking tartan, fucking bagpipes'. In his work he re-imagined the whole of Scotland's history into a much more bludgeoned and brutal fantasy than the romantic myths which litter popular culture.

A NEW TARTAN TRUTH

Thus, McQueen's AW95 collection was a shout-out against so many other English designers. Where before there had been more luxuriant, flamboyant creations from the likes of Vivienne Westwood, he honed

ruthlessly in on the oppression and anger of a nation. Refusing to use the kilt, the doublet or the plaid as a basis, McQueen focused on form and shape to convey not the rape of the female body, but England's rape of Scotland.

Naturally, though, the pundits and the media looked only at the obvious. With models wearing slashed garments that exposed their breasts and their usual easy stride replaced with, in some cases, the stagger of one who has been brutalised, it was easy to cease critical thinking at the surface.

Highland Rape marked the point at which McQueen as a designer crossed the boundaries of political poetry and startling form, making this collection more art than fashion.

McQueen's critics accused him of misogyny, but he was simply challenging convention. He commented that it didn't matter whether the spectator was repulsed or inspired, as long as his work evoked emotion then to him it was a success. The underlying fact was that although the Highland Rape garments were savagely cut to expose flesh, and there was a harshness to the blood red and gothic black of the tartan, McQueen combined this with chiffon and lace giving voice, too, to notions of fragility. Models were styled with dark eye make-up and mirrored contact lenses; through this dark blankness of the 'victim' there radiated an inherent strength where women were displayed not as meek and vulnerable but as fearless and fervent.

THE WIDOWS OF CULLODEN

In 2006 McQueen's collection stood as an artistic memorial – and familial tribute, and perhaps a nod towards which way the McQueen family's own allegiances lay – to all widows who had lost their husbands in the Jacobite uprising. Entitled 'The Widows of Culloden', it marked a return after more than a decade to a theatrical delivery for a collection. The provocative soundtrack combined the piano, Highland drums and bagpipes mixed with punk rock and echoes of the howling Scottish wind.

In terms of design, its edge was slightly more commercial, with the violence of Highland Rape replaced by more fluid lines. There were draped tartans with dramatic waistlines, black lace and plumes of grouse and partridge. The MacQueen tartan was bias cut in dress panels to disguise the pattern and also define the female form. The detailing in each design was incredible; this was less art and more craft.

McQueen had enlisted Philip Treacy and Shaun Leane to create beautifully exquisite head-dresses to accent the garments. The most notable was a bird's nest edged with taxidermy mallard wings with seven blue speckled eggs encrusted with Swarovski crystals – the fragile eggs tilting forward as if about to tumble out . . .

The more commercial aspects of the Widows of Culloden collection point towards a feeling of heirloom pieces, where the garment holds its own emotional significance. In these designs, McQueen directed attention away from the conflict

of the earlier collection and towards the beauty of more technically rich pieces inspired by traditional Scottish costume. Bustles and bell skirts were combined with military-style doublets. In stark contrast to the ideals from his first Highland fling, McQueen took a more settled approach: he seemed to be shunning visions of shock and brutality in favour of a 'considered' look, with its focus on gothic opulence to offer a grander, more refined and immaculately crafted view of a modern Scotland.

A RARE MCQUEEN KILT

It is worth noting that McQueen never designed a kilt for a menswear collection, and one of the rare times he was seen sporting one was at the Metropolitan

Museum of Art's gala benefit dinner in New York in 2006. It was traditional formal Highland wear, but with the McQueen twist of patent black fetish-inspired ghillie brogues and half collar untucked white shirt under a black Bonnie Prince Charlie jacket. His accessory for the evening was Sarah Jessica Parker daringly, stunningly draped in a huge MacQueen tartan silk sash over a nude chiffon and black lace dress. Photos of the two clasping hands portray an ironic image of a displaced Scottish Islander in the land of the displaced, at a time in his stellar career when McQueen was beginning to question his own motives and his own persona.

A DARK AND GOTHIC TARTAN

As much as Westwood had used tartan as a punk cry of rebellion, then in her 'Anglomania' as a show of opulent exaggeration, McQueen focused less on tartan's romance and more on Scotland's troubled, complex history. It's a history that, in the main, tartan has deftly masked and side-stepped since the time of Sir Walter Scott's Pageant. With unflinching artistry, McQueen used the darkly gothic to shock and articulate a Scottish reality that positioned tartan as far away from a shortbread tin as it could get.

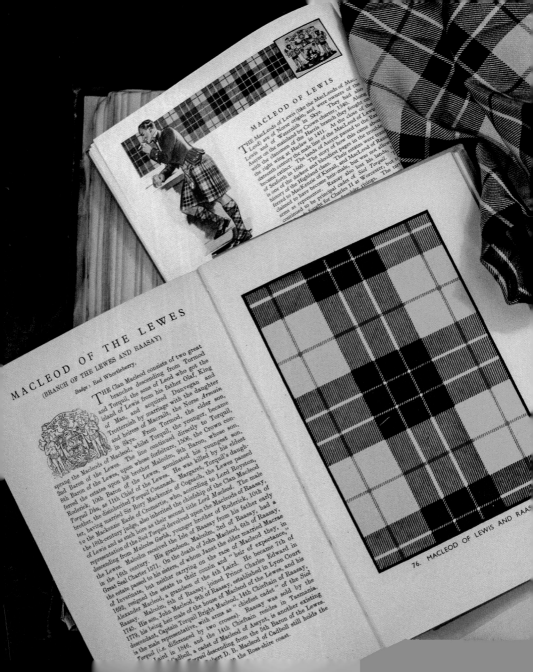

MACLEOD OF THE LEWES
(BRANCH OF THE LEWES AND RAASAY)

Badge : Red Whortleberry.

THE Clan Macleod consists of two great branches descending from Tormod and Torquil, the sons of Leod who got the island of Lewis from his father Olaf, King of Man, and acquired Dunvegan and Trotternish by marriage with the daughter and heiress of Macraill, the Norse *Armin* in Skye. From Tormod, the elder son, *Torquil Dhu*, whilst Torquil, the younger, became 2nd Baron of the Lewes. The line continued directly to Torquil, 8th Baron of the Lewes, upon whose forfeiture, 1506, the Crown conferred the estates upon his brother Malcolm, 9th Baron, whose son, Roderick, 10th Baron of the Lewes. He was killed by his eldest brother, the disinherited *Torquil Conanach*, Margaret, Torquil's daughter, having married Sir Rory Mackenzie of Cogeach, the Lewes passed to the Mackenzie Earls of Cromartie, who, according to the Clan Macleod of the 18th-century judge, also inherited the chiefship of the Clan Macleod of Lewis and as such bore as their second title *Lord Macleod*. The male representation from *Malcolm Garbh*, younger brother of Roderick, 10th of the Lewes. Malcolm received the Isle of Raasay from his father early in the 16th century. His grandson, Malcolm, 3rd of Raasay, had a Great Seal Charter 1571. On the death of Janet the elder married Macrae of Inverinate, the estate passed to his sisters, carrying on the race of Macleod they, in 1692, resigned the estate to their cousin, a "heir of expectance," Alexander Macleod, a grandson of the 4th Laird. He became 7th of Raasay. Malcolm, 5th of Raasay, joined Prince Charles Edward in 1745. His son, John Macleod, 9th of Raasay, established in Lyon Court 1779, his being heir male of the house of Macleod of the Lewes, and his descendant, Captain Torquil Bright Macleod, 14th Chieftain of the *Siol Torquil* (i.e. differenced with arms as " chiefest cadet " of the *Siol* Laird in 1846, and the 14th Chieftain resides in Tasmania. Torquil (i.e. differenced by two crosses). Raasay was sold by the is the male representative, with arms as " chiefest cadet " of the *Siol* ... Cadboll, a cadet of Macleod of Assynt, is another existing ... bert T. D. B. Macleod of Cadboll still holds the ... descending from the 5th Baron of the Lewes. ... Ross-shire coast.

MACLEOD OF LEWIS

THE MacLeods of Lewis (like the MacLeods of Mac Leod) are of Waternish in Skye. They had also Lewis on the mainland by Crown charter, 1340. Along with the clansmen of the Harris branch they fought on the right wing at Harlaw in 1411. At the close of the sixteenth century the male line of the MacLeod of the Lewe became extinct. The lands of Assynt passed to the about of Seaforth in 1660. The story of how this came about is one of the darkest and bloodiest pages in the troubled history of the Highland clans. These estates were transferred to Mackenzie of Kintail, and MacLeod of Raasay claimed to have become heir-male, but was not allowed arms as representor. Raasay also lost his lands, continued to be principal cadet of *Siol Torquil* ... fought for Charles II at Worcester, but ... hire risings. The tart

HISTORY

TARTAN
Gordon

Rep blue
Rep black
Rep yellow
Rep green

Highland Dress

Self Measurement Form

from

STEWART, CHRISTIE & C?
86, GEORGE STREET,
EDINBURGH

EVENING DRESS, MONTROSE DOUBLET

THE KILT . . .

There I've said it. That's this chapter over, one kilt, one Scotland.

But we all know that is not strictly true. In fact, there's a truth, one that's been hidden, lost – or ignored – and forgotten in some decidedly Scottish mists of time. The kilt as we know it today was designed by an Englishman. Yes, that's right. A Sassenach from south of the border was responsible for creating the epitome of modern Scottish dress. It's a wonder that any self-respecting Scotsman would see fit to don such a garment . . .

But what we're talking about is the modern kilt, a garment I reflect on later. I just wanted to start the chapter with a shocker to whet your appetite; I couldn't quite believe it when I read it either.

THE NON-MODERN KILT

The kilt started life as a less than refined garment. While first evidence of the kilt's current style can be found in the 1500s, the tradition of the kilt surely reaches further back than that. Chamber's Twentieth Century Dictionary, published in 1901, tells us:

> *Kilt, kilt,* n. a man's short petticoat or plaited skirt, part of a highlandman's dress. – v.t. to truss up, to pleat vertically. – v.i. to go lightly, trip. – adj. *kilt'ed* dressed in a kilt: tucked up: vertically pleated. – n. kilt'y, kilt'ie, a wearer of a kilt [Scand.; cf. Dan. Kilte, to tuck up; O.N. Kilting a skirt.]

Many sources claim the etymology of 'kilt' is actually Scandinavian, derived from an Old Norse word '*kjalta*' that means the 'fold of a gathered skirt', and the derivation of '*kilte*' meaning to 'tuck up'. But, putting words to one side, there is no doubt that the Gaelic '*fèileadh-mòr*' – the great plaid – and the '*breacan-an-fhèilidh*' – the belted plaid – were the early ancestors in fabric form of the kilt as we know it today.

UNDER THE KILT

The old question of 'What does a Scotsman wear under his kilt?' has its own origins too. In Pictish times the day-to-day outer garment for a man was simply a long shirt, the tails of which were about knee length. This was called a '*lèine-chròich*',

and it was created from an ochre yellow dyed linen. A tunic-like garment, it was made from up to nine metres of linen. Clearly, this is a lot of cloth for a shirt; a modern shirt takes about two metres. So, working from this, the simple answer to the under-the-kilt question is surely 'Nothing', as the tunic did act simply like an underskirt. My guess is that a tunic shirt was wrapped in a similar fashion to the belted plaid, but was topped with a *fèileadh-mòr* acting more like a woollen cape for protection from the elements.

TARTAN UNDERGARMENTS

Fast forward to Victorian times, and to the dress of Mr John Brown, the queen's aide at Balmoral. The National Museum of Scotland holds two pairs of rough tartan flannel boxer shorts that once belonged to Mr Brown. One pair are terribly moth-eaten (obviously his favourites?), and the second are in near pristine condition (saved for best?). Such undergarments were a sensible move to ensure the winds from the north did not expose Queen Victoria to some unexpected flesh. Perhaps, too, they ensured Mr Brown felt suitably decent in royal company. Ah, my romance is destroyed.

THE FÈILEADH-MÒR

The 1600s saw an evolved form of the 'Big Wrap' – which is, of course, yet another name for the 'great plaid'. As referenced in *Outlander,* there's a proper way to don a *fèileadh-mòr*! First, take your cloth and lay it out on the ground. Then pleat it while it's flat. Next lie on the cloth and fold, tuck and wrap it around your waist and fasten with a belt. Then you stand up and throw the rest over your shoulders and around your torso. Clearly, it's not the easiest garment to put on in a hurry, and I'm guessing that during the cold days of winter it would rarely be removed at all.

I envisage this great plaid as a more functional form of an oversized cape, one that takes 8.3 metres (or nine old-school yards), and what we call today the 'full width' of cloth at 138 cm (or 54 inches). These impressive dimensions required two lengths of cloth to be joined together, as an old crofter's loom could only produce up to 70 cm for the width of the tartan. In a dense woven wool, these proportions create a fair weight of cloth, cumbersome and heavy. My guess is that thanks to the dreich Scottish weather and boggy landscapes it was wise not to have anything below the knee; for freedom of movement and to avoid being clad in wet wool with no guarantees as to when you might be able to dry it.

And the lack of below-the-knee wear included hose, which came later for the Highlanders. With their bare legs and untanned shoes of deerskin, the Highland Scots were called 'Redshanks' by their lowland neighbours.

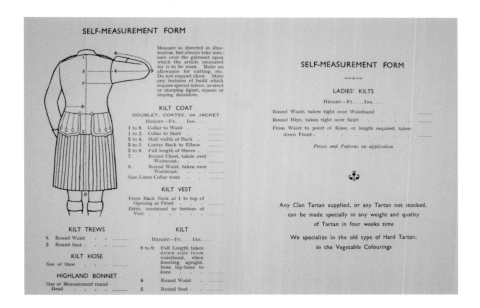

THE PRACTICAL SIDE OF KILTS

Before technical outdoor gear was a thing, the *fèileadh-mòr* was a practical piece of kit if you were out in the wilds herding cattle. It's a garment which could protect you from the elements but be unfurled into a sleeping bag too.

In 1582, the renowned humanist scholar George Buchanan, wrote a 'concise' history of Scotland named *Rerum Scoticarum Historia*. In talking about the Highlanders, he referred to their striped cloth. His words would indicate that it was perhaps some time before the cross weave came into effect, meaning that the stripe ran the length of the cloth along the warp.

They delight in variegated garments, especially striped, and their favourite colours are purple and blue. Their ancestors wore plaids of many different colours, and numbers still retain this custom, but the majority, now, in their dress prefer a dark brown, imitating nearly the leaves of the heather, that when lying upon the heath in the day, they may not be discovered by the appearance of their clothes; in these, wrapped rather than covered, they brave the severest storms in the open air, and sometimes lay themselves down to sleep even in the midst of snow.

The dark brown colours used for hunting were more like modern-day camouflage. It was also noted that the wool used was coarse but tightly woven to make it midge proof, and with so much lanolin still in the fleece this made it water-repellent too.

The plaid evolved over time, as did the tartan itself. This was driven by advancements in weaving and looms, and by the colouring from natural dyes. Dyes from far-off shores became available as trading with the east saw all manner of new shades – for example, rich reds from Turkey

known as 'Edirne Red' – emerged. Carpet and rug weaving were common crafts in the Ottoman empire at this time, and they led the way in natural dye production. Using different parts of the plant or the whole above-ground plant they were able to create around ten different colours.

However, the biggest leap was the creation of the *fèileadh-beag* or philibeg, which roughly translated means 'little wrap' or 'little kilt'. This, as mentioned, was – scandal! – the invention of a man from Lancashire.

A HIGHLAND INROAD

So, some historical context is useful at this point. After the first Jacobite uprising of 1715, the British government appointed General George Wade as Commander-in-Chief of Scotland. At least one part of his job was the unenviable task of keeping the clans in order. Doing this wasn't made any easier by the lack of roads, or proper tracks in Scotland at the time, so General Wade decided to improve links between communities by building lots of new roads. His highways project started in 1726 and was completed in 1740, no doubt late and over budget, as is always the way.

These roads made the Highlands more accessible to industry and the military. One of the early investors into this road-building idea was Thomas Rawlinson, an ironmaster of Quaker roots from Lancashire. Very little is recorded of Rawlinson, but more light can be cast on his business partner Iain MacDonnell, head of the Glengarry family. Their foundry was built just outside of Inverness at Invergarry, and employed MacDonnell clansman, who – used to more outdoors pursuits – wore their cumbersome *fèileadh-mòr* to the foundry, which unsurprisingly hampered their work there.

Such work included cutting lumber and stoking furnaces for smelting iron, all of which was a little different from roaming across the glens. And it meant that the workers' attire seemed to be impeding the foundry's efficiency: simply put, their garb was getting in the way. So Rawlinson took it upon himself to approach a military tailor in Inverness, a man called Parkinson, to translate the clansmen's plaid into workwear. That must have been some conversation: 'Aye, somethin' a wee bit less flappy perhaps, Mr Rawlinson?'

THE KILT TAKES A NEW SHAPE

Mr Parkinson's response to the brief was to simply remove the top half of the plaid, keep the lower portion and set the pleats firmly in position by stitching them in place, all fastened up with side buckles. This does beg the question: if this task was given to a military tailor were there Highland regiments already wearing something less cumbersome than the great plaid? Or was it the other way round – did this tailor of Inverness actually start a revolution?

Either way, the invention caught on and by 1745 the well-dressed Highland gentleman's wardrobe consisted of:

- tartan kilt
- belted plaid
- tartan jacket
- tartan waistcoat
- pair of tartan trews
- pair of woollen stockings
- necessary garters
- plus a couple of pairs of brogues*

For all you hipsters, the broguing refers to the punched holes which formed a pattern on the shoes. These originally had the practical purpose of allowing water to escape from the shoe while walking.

TREWS MADE OF TARTAN

Now, for those of you ticking this list off, you will have spotted trews, a garment that's been around at least as long as the kilt.

The year 1355 marks the earliest record of trews – as detailed in the accounting records for Lord John of the Isles. And a couple of hundred years later the ledger for King James V shows 'three ells of highland tartan' to make trousers. Since the seventh century AD, in Pictish times, it was always the head of the village who would wear the trousers. These showed their status in the hierarchy, and could well be the origin of the phrase, 'Who wears the trousers?'

Today at Stewart Christie & Co. we make eight times more pairs of tartan trousers than we do kilts; the trews really are an emerging trend for the younger gentleman. Their versatility is one reason for their popularity, depending on where and when the tartan trousers are to be worn. If they are for evening wear, then trousers travel far more easily. It's much more straightforward to pack a pair of trews and a dinner – or velvet – jacket for a black-tie event than it is to squash a kilt and all the regalia which accompanies it into your leather holdall.

Furthermore, tartan trews seems to be more acceptable – and a stronger fashion statement south of the border too. The current trend is for a slimmer-cut leg, which echoes the contemporary silhouette of 'skinny' trousers. While the shape and length of men's trousers or breeches have seen quite dramatic changes throughout history, the style for tartan has remained that of a close-fitting shape on the leg – lending them a timelessly on-trend and stylish look.

THE ART OF A MILITARY CUT

Proper military-cut trews are a true art form in their own right; to make them properly a tailor needs to use almost as much tartan as for a kilt, with a lot of wastage. The reason for this is that the military-cut requires a 'one piece' leg, meaning there is no side seam like you would see on everyday trousers. Instead, it is one continuous piece of cloth wrapping each leg, which poses problems when it comes to matching the check exactly on the seat and the front fork. Few people are what one might call a standard shape and that's where the artistry of cutting these military trews comes into its own.

TO GO WITH THE KILT

Since the 1800s there have been some pretty solid rules about what you can wear with your kilt, for what occasion and under what circumstances . . . or so tailors would have you believe. Until very recently, it could be argued that it's always been the task of nobility and royalty to bend and create their own rules when it comes to dress, leaving the rest of us to conform to the established rules and fashions. If we take a closer look at these rules it would seem that in reality very little has actually changed since the 1860s when it comes to Highland dress.

BUCKINGHAM PALACE.

18th May, 1953.

Dear Sir,

The Duke of Edinburgh has asked me to thank you for your letter enclosing a copy of your new Handbook on Highland Dress, and to say how much he appreciates your kindness in sending it to him.

Yours truly,

B. Marling

Equerry-in-Waiting to
The Duke of Edinburgh

Messrs. Stewart, Christie & Co.,
86 George Street,
Edinburgh 2.

THE IMPORTANCE OF BEING CORRECT

At Stewart Christie, we have a lovely collection of old catalogues from which we take the guides and look back to see what would have been deemed 'correct' dress in the early part of the 20th century.

My favourite is one from the 1940s which outlines all the types of correct formal Highland dress for all occasions from court levees, evening state parties, evening dress, afternoon dress and outdoor dress. It offers a very concise but specific description of the kilt, which I would like to share with you.

The Kilt
The tartan is usually supplied bearing the name of the wearer or the clan to which he belongs. In many cases his

name may be associated with the name of the clan, or as a sept to a certain clan. If the wearer has no particular claim to a tartan, it is frequently found that the name on the maternal side may furnish a clue, failing that, the Caledonia or the different Stewart tartans may be worn, or the Culloden or Jacobite tartans are permitted to be used. The length of the kilt should be to the centre of the knee when standing erect, or to clear the ground when kneeling, and should hang practically at the same level back and front. Our clients may rely upon getting an excellent fitting kilt which will hang well, as all our kilts are made by skilled kiltmakers.

The catalogue continues with all the additional 'accoutrements' to complete the look for each and every occasion. If you add these up, it's clear that it was not a cheap endeavour to make sure you were suitably dressed. The idea of the *fèileadh-mòr* translates into 'modern' Highland dress as the long belted plaid and the long shoulder plaid.

The Long Shoulder plaid, otherwise known as a Scarf Plaid, should be folded twice the long way of the plaid, and then doubled across and over the left shoulder, doubled edge to left, fringe to reach about the level of the waist; then carry one end back over shoulder to right, under right arm, and across the chest over left shoulder under the other portion

of plaid. Then opened out to cover the left arm. The lower part of the plaid should not hang below the lowest edge of the kilt.

However often you read this it doesn't get any easier to follow! You have to be wearing one to fully appreciate how to thread and wear it. The belted plaid is slightly lighter and simpler, as follows.

The belted plaid is fastened by the strap round the waist under the waistcoat, and top end to left shoulder by a silk cord attached to the shoulder strap button, and firmly secured by a shoulder brooch. This short plaid is lighter to wear and can be taken off whilst dancing. The lower part of the plaid should hang below the lowest edge of the kilt.

And once you've dealt with all that, there is a whole list of other pieces to complete the look, including:

- full dress tartan hose
- shoulder brooch
- the sporran and sporran strap
- the Highland sword
- the cross belt
- *sgian-dubh*
- kilt pin
- jabot
- cuffs
- dress shoes, *and*
- Highland bonnet

BONNETS, RIBBONS AND FAVOURS

Strange as it might sound, the Highland bonnet is a piece of tartan history that transcends gender. But, for the most part, when it comes to tartan there is a plethora of references as to how men might wear it best, but little in the way for us ladies. Evidence suggests that tartan was always predominantly a masculine cloth and Highland ladies would wear it to show support of, and a sense of identity with, their clan or their beau.

Descriptions of early styles of layered dresses exist, but they were short – hitched between the knee and the ankle to stop the hems dragging in the mud – 'kilted' some might say: a practical style for Highland life. But these features were common to most country clothing of the age. When tartan was included in women's clothes it was used for Sunday best, or as a detail – with tartan ribbon added to dresses as fastenings – or simply as favours or decoration.

Tartan would also have mostly been used for women's shawls or earasaids, which were larger more blanket-like shawls. For formal occasions, a tartan sash would show your clan, either in wool or in silk for evening dress. As we have seen, of all the varieties of tartan, the Dress tartan was classed as the ladies' tartan; with its predominantly white background the set definitely has a more feminine feel to it.

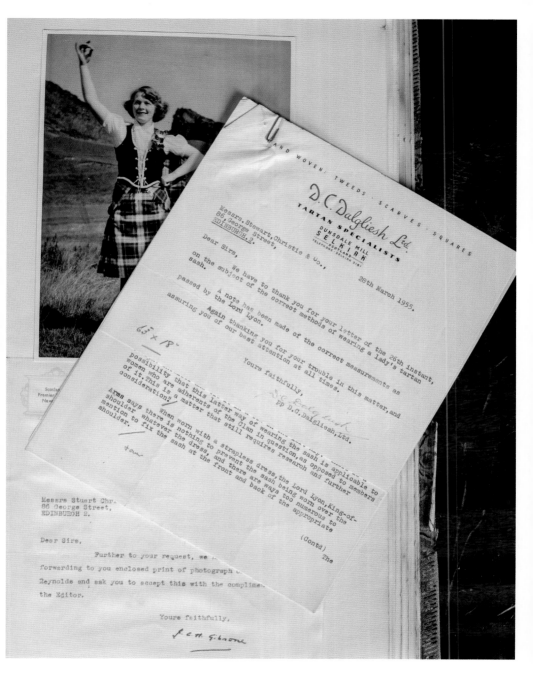

AND WOVEN: TWEEDS · SCARVES · SQUARES

D.C. Dalgliesh Ltd.
TARTAN SPECIALISTS
DUNSDALE MILL
SELKIRK
SCOTLAND

28th March 1955.

Messrs. Stewart, Christie & Co.,
86 George Street,
EDINBURGH. 2.

Dear Sirs,

We have to thank you for your letter of the 26th instant, on the subject of the correct methods of wearing a lady's tartan sash.

A note has been made of the correct measurements as passed by the Lord Lyon.

Again thanking you for your trouble in this matter, and assuring you of our best attention at all times,

Yours faithfully,

D.C. Dalgliesh
pp D.C. Dalgliesh, Ltd.

63" x 18"

possibility that this latter way of wearing the sash is applicable to women who are adherents of the Clan in question, as opposed to members of it, this is a matter that still requires research and further consideration.

Arms says there is nothing to prevent the sash being worn over the shoulder, whatever the dress, and there are ways too numerous to mention to fix the sash at the front and back of the appropriate shoulder.

When worn with a strapless dress, the Lord Lyon, King-of-

(Contd)

The

Messrs Stuart Chr.
86 George Street,
EDINBURGH E.

Dear Sirs,

Further to your request, we
forwarding to you enclosed print of photograph
Reynolds and ask you to accept this with the complimen
the Editor.

Yours faithfully,

J.C.H. Gibsone

THE TARTAN DRESS

Some amazing examples of tartan ladies' dress exist, but they date more from the late Hanoverian period to the Victorian era. The chances are they were only worn a couple of times – perhaps one reason why they've survived? After all a tartan dress makes quite a statement – it's guaranteed to cut a dash – and in polite society you wouldn't want to be seen wearing 'that dress' again! Even so, the romantic notion of lassies in those long tartan dresses with their tight corset-style bodices still seems to linger in our minds.

This myth persists, but the truth for Highland dancers – who actually wear tartan in dress form – is that their outfits were devised in the 1970s to create a standardised look, a shift which had nothing to do with history other than ideas distilled from tartan, a need for practicality and ease of movement. Previously, Highland solo dancers and sword dancers had adopted a curious tradition of wearing men's kilts, jackets and bonnets to dance in.

Today – luckily for them – their dancing uniform is one that consists of: knee-length kilt in dress tartan, white shirt, tartan sash, tight-fitted bodice or waistcoat in complementary velvet, *and* a pair of white (not cream) knee-length plain hose.

Our historical recollections indicate that it wasn't until the Victorian era that tartan dresses became the widely sought-after look of *La Mode Ecosse*. But even when in vogue, these dresses were a mythical reproduction of the idealised form they had taken on in the previous century. Reinvented, romanticised and redefined, it's not until the latter part of the 19th century that tartan became a cloth worn more by women than by men in the world of mainstream fashion.

AN UNDERLYING MYTH

But all this tartan chat hasn't answered the eternal question of what a Scotsman wears under his kilt?

The answer should be *nothing*, giving extra kudos to that myth of sexy ruggedness . . . but, really, was that ever a secret?

M A C R A E

Slogan :—" Sgùr Urain " (A mountain in Kintail).

Badge :—Garbhag an t-slèibhe (Fir Club Moss).

IT is generally understood that the
Macrae—Gaelic MacRath
Grace," and had, in all
cal origin "...

THE CLAN MACRAE

War Cry :—" Sgùr Urain " (A mountain in Kintail).

Badge :—Garbhag an t-slèibhe (Fir Club Moss).

It is generally understood that the name Macrae—Gaelic Mac-Rath—means "Son of Grace," and had in all probability an ecclesiastical origin. It occurs as a personal or Christian name in Ireland, and also in Scotland, from the fifth to the fourteenth century. It was common as a surname in the fifteenth and sixteenth century, and south of Perthshire in the sixteenth century, and is still common, with various forms of the spelling—M'Crie, M'Cra, M'Creath, etc.

"The home of the Highland Clan Macrae, sometimes called "The Wild Macrae," was Kintail, in Ross-shire, where they are said to have migrated from the Lovat country. The late Con-they were originally a Morayshire clan, which sounded westward. Their surname, according to the Macrae arms corrob-orate to this origin, its similarity to high position it occupies in the whose ablest and most loyal supporters the MacKenzie Barons of Kintail, and so became largely the means of raising them to power, and to wards the Earldom of Seaforth. The Macraes were Chamberlains of the annals of Scottish history. To high position it occupies in the public and for many generations. The Macraes frequently Vicars of the Gable of Eilean-Donan Castle, restored that ancient stronghold John Macrae.

Rev. Farquhar Macrae (1580-1662) was Vicar of Kintail for forty-four years. One of his sons, Rev. John Macrae of Dingwall (1614-1673), who took a prominent part in the ecclesiastical controversies of the time, was progenitor of the Macraes of Conchra, a family that has been honourably represented in the British army for several generations.

The Rev. John A. Macrae, son of the late Sir Colin Macrae, who claimed him as Chief before Lyon Court in 1909, was the representative of the House of Inverinate.

... is the present ... ter of Inverinate.

Eilean-Donan.

ARCHIVE

TARTAN
Macrae

Anc green
Anc blue
Black
Anc scarlet
Bleached white

SCHOOL DAYS

When I first took ownership of Stewart Christie, it was apparent that the knowledge I had amassed over my career in clothing was useful, but I still had a lot to learn – and I mean a lot. A steep curve was ahead of me. Stewart Christie had survived uprisings, wars, changes to the throne and to government in its three centuries, and at each turn it steadfastly clung to the need for handmade, high-quality attire. My first day felt like I was going back to school, to a very old school, steeped in history and full of unfamiliar rules, expectations and protocols.

The history itself wasn't my natural milieu, either. It's not that I ever found history boring exactly, but I've found it needs to hold some sense of relevance or relatability for me to find it truly interesting. I loved stories as a child, and I admit I do love antiques, but the thought of a history lesson failed to fill me with any enthusiasm – a mass of timelines and

deeds, which had to be learned and held no bearing on my own life. I preferred to be enveloped by history, not simply taught it. I love it when someone shares their passion for a historical era – it will always inspire me – it brings a perspective and humanity to what would otherwise be dry words and dates on a page.

THE OLD KID ON THE BLOCK

So, on that first day, I entered a company with nearly three hundred years of history – and it was the longevity of their presence in Scotland that suddenly made history more real, more touchable, to me. Stewart Christie & Co. is the oldest bespoke tailors in Scotland, still making garments on the original premises and serving 'Gentry, Nobility and Royalty' as one of the old newspaper adverts reads, something which is as true today as it was back in 1910.

The company was founded in 1720, under the name of Marshall Aitken, in

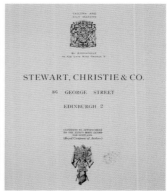

premises opposite St Giles' Cathedral on what is now the Royal Mile. In August 1745 the shop staff and tailors would have seen the Jacobite uprising march past their shopfront on the way to the castle. It must have been strange to them – would it have been scary, or exhilarating? – and it certainly feels strange to me now, knowing that the company saw part of the Jacobite era. It gives me a huge sense of pride to have that connection with such significant historical events.

I always joke that we are merely looking after Stewart Christie for the next generation, and I think this feeling was instilled in, and by, the previous owner. His family owned the company for four generations and, having no children to take it on after him, I believe he felt passionately about passing his legacy on to a safe set of hands. This might sound romantic, but I now finally understand the importance of this – we are continuing a tradition, safeguarding the second-oldest business in Edinburgh.

A TARTAN TIME WARP

When we first took over Stewart Christie, we were overflowing with radical ideas on how to modernise and breathe new life into it. The shop felt stuck in the 1970s – a far from ideal time warp; style-wise, we would have preferred the 1870s. Nevertheless, we soon came to realise that we needed to be respectful, considerate and build on what we already had. It was vital that our ambition was not about change but about evolution. But how? When we accessed the company archive, we soon saw that it offered the ideal resource for this.

The clothing archive was our first port

of call. It was a curious mixture of tailcoats, robes and ceremonial wear, but sadly no tartan pieces. The real history of Stewart Christie turned out to be encapsulated in six volumes of handwritten ledgers – a mixture of notes on styles and various pieces, the company's early PR strategy. The jigsaw of drawings and photos and letters formed a rich weave of stories. Going through the archives made me feel like an archaeologist, picking out, dusting off and interpreting lost tales of garments long since worn. Unsurprisingly, we discovered a few tales about tartan.

TARTAN IN PRINT

In one of the last archives – the final one dates from the late 1950s – we made a curious discovery. An advert in an old newspaper article states:

> *Illustrated book of tartans over 100 years old. Authenticated tartans of the clans and families of Scotland, illustrations painted by machinery (mauchline process) published first in 1850 [by Andrew and William Smith] . . . available for clients to see in the month of May [at Stewart Christie & Co.].*

I found this exact copy of *Authenticated Tartans of the Clan and Families of Scotland* in the shop, and unless you know what it is then it doesn't look like much, but my joy when I found it – *wow!* Now I know how archaeologists feel when they find an ancient gold necklace under a mound of dirt.

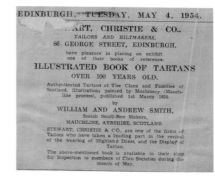

EDINBURGH, TUESDAY, MAY 4, 1954.

..ART, CHRISTIE & CO.,
TAILORS AND KILTMAKERS,
86 GEORGE STREET, EDINBURGH,
have pleasure in placing on exhibit
one of their books of reference.

ILLUSTRATED BOOK OF TARTANS
OVER 100 YEARS OLD.

Authenticated Tartans of The Clans and Families of Scotland, illustrations painted by Machinery (Mauchline process), published 1st March 1850.
by
WILLIAM AND ANDREW SMITH,
Scotch Snuff-Box Makers,
MAUCHLINE, AYRSHIRE, SCOTLAND.

STEWART, CHRISTIE & CO., are one of the firms of Tailors who have taken a leading part in the revival of the wearing of Highland Dress, and the Display of Tartan.

The above-mentioned book is available in their shop for inspection to members of Clan Societies during the month of May.

EVENING DRESS, PRINCE CHARLIE COATEE

Stewart, Christie & Co., Edinburgh

Examples of the Smith's tartan ware—a calendar for the French market (left); a book cover with a view of Edinburgh Castle (centre); probably the 'ladies' companion' referred to in the Smith correspondence (right); and, in front, a spectacle-case, pencil and parasol handle.

Fern pattern ware of about 1900, the last attempt by the Smiths to establish a new fashion. Left to right, a tartan holder; a tea caddy; decorated by Miller's secret process; and a photographic label applied to a tartan "court plaister" case.

The book features 69 colour plates, all of the unique clan tartans present at the time of writing in 1850. This book was possibly the first time tartan, in all its glory, had ever been recorded in print – all other references up until this point show tartan only ever as a woven cloth.

TWO TARTAN BROTHERS

Its authors, brothers William and Andrew Smith from Mauchline in Ayrshire, were established pioneers of 'Tartan Ware' or 'Mauchline Ware' (pronounced Moch'lin) items at the time of publication. Since the 1820s, they had been producing wooden – sycamore – boxes of various uses and sizes and 'drawing' images onto the wood. Capitalising on the booming tourist trade stemming from Queen Victoria's passion for Scotland, the Smiths' companies, by 1850, were producing tartan-patterned products, souvenirs for those visitors seeking to take a piece of Scotland home with them.

A newspaper article from 1954 discusses how intriguing the book really was as the printing technique used to record the tartan was unique to the Smith brothers. Their machinery would draw one line of ink at a time – creating a very similar effect to the weaving of tartan. The Smiths' factory was destroyed in a fire in 1933, which saw an end to the family's tartan-related dominance. The fashion for these items has long since passed, so it's not surprising that some of the techniques might have been lost.

Personally, the book was a startling revelation about the accessibility of the history of tartan to the general public. Up until that point, I'd always made the assumption that there has always been an accurate printed record of the core tartans, designs, or setts, freely available for people to reference. But it seems this was not the case.

TO TARTAN OR NOT TO TARTAN?

Another article we found in our exploration of the Stewart Christie & Co. archive, which dates from 1953, states that knowledge of the correctness for Highland dress had been lost. I had simply assumed there had always been strict guides in place with regards to the wearing of the kilt, which had been in existence since the pageant of 1822, but again I was incorrect. The article we unearthed debates the proper wearing of Highland dress for specific occasions and whether or not an individual was 'entitled' to wear tartan. Living in the age we are now, with all of tartan's thousands of variations, and myriad corporate tartans too, it is easy to forget that there was once a distinct and stolid pride in the fact that you – as a Highland Scot – had the specific right to wear the cloth.

I half dismissed the article until I came across a stack of brochures, some photographic, some fashion drawings and a lot of text on rough paper, neatly stashed away in a sealed box. On closer inspection, I saw that they were reference guides on what to wear and how to wear it! As the date was June 1953, I assume there must have been some controversy around the queen's coronation and her arrival in Scotland to attend state functions. Perhaps the Stewart Christie & Co. designers of the 1950s took the initiative to lay down a new set of guidelines for wearing Highland dress in the modern age.

As Stewart Christie were responsible for compiling this guide, I can only imagine they were either best positioned with their client base to record the details or perhaps they just wanted to go the extra mile and win back their royal warrant which had been lost with the death of HRH George V. I say this because there is a letter from Buckingham Palace in the bound book thanking Stewart Christie for forwarding a copy of the booklet to the Duke of Edinburgh, and a further letter thanking the company for offering their services to the Queen's husband (see page 184).

If you were in the military at that time, a guide would have been superfluous as there already were specific outfits for specific occasions, but for the royals and upper classes – and the aspiring middle classes – it was the definitive guide for those wanting to wear tartan in the correct fashion. After reading further articles and newspaper clippings, I was amused to discover how essential it in fact was. After all, 'a gentleman was seen sporting a bowler hat with his kilt' – how thoroughly modern!

FITTED OUT FOR THE EMPIRE EXHIBITION

Delving further into the records, I found reference to the Empire Exhibition held in Glasgow in 1938. A similar idea to Prince Albert's Great Exhibition in London's Crystal Palace in 1851, it celebrated and attempted to boost Scottish industry after the Depression of the 1930s. It was attended by over six million visitors, who enjoyed pavilions, open-air gardens and fairground rides in what is now Bellahouston Park. Stewart Christie & Co. were invited to create an outfit to showcase; an outfit which was both innovative and displayed the skills of their craft.

The company chose to make two pieces: a very precise double-breasted business suit and a second, rather

more creative, tartan outfit. The Stewart Christie & Co. archive contains letters and descriptions of this latter outfit. It was a distinctly Scottish evening ensemble, made from the most expensive materials of the time, and consisted of a pair of pure cashmere tartan trews matched with a plain cashmere smoking jacket with tartan satin lapels. It all sounds pretty ordinary and looks very subtle in the black and white photo of the exhibit . . . until I turned the page and found its design cuttings. The description is as follows:

Finest blue cashmere double-breasted smoking jacket, lined scarlet silk serge contrasting straw station sleeve lining. Red Fraser tartan silk roll collar, facings and cuffs, the tartan silk representing the old colours of the tartan. The entire jacket braided in red and blue silk cord with olivets in red ground covered with blue netting, cut to a 40 inch chest, waist 33 1/2", length 31" to button 2 with two outside pockets one outside vertical pocket.

Soft pure Cashmere Tartan Trousers, the Tartan in the old colours with silk cord girdle in blue and red, cut to a 34" waist, two side pockets. Trousers cut without a side seam, and lined in scarlet silk serge.

It seems no expense was spared on the outfit. Feeling the swatches, the cashmere is of the softest texture, but also carries a fair weight. I am amazed that the trousers hold a crease as the cloth is incredibly tactile. The colours are vibrant, and I can imagine the whole outfit would have been deeply comfortable as loungewear, but potentially delightfully warm too, ideal for wearing around a draughty Scottish castle.

The one-piece leg pattern on the tartan trousers would have used a lot more fabric than a standard trouser and been

complicated to cut. Looking at the photo you see the sett falling straight down the crease and matching through perfectly, so from a professional point of view it is a particularly well-executed piece of tailoring.

A BUSINESS PARTNERSHIP

One person who's shared my Stewart Christie journey is my business partner, Daniel Fearn. His personal style makes him slightly more at ease with taking on the responsibility of three hundred years of tailoring. In our research together, we discovered many hidden stories and company facts which had perhaps been forgotten about over the years. Daniel and I share a passion for hand-crafted, locally made cloth and garments, and together we embarked on defining Stewart Christie for a new generation.

Q&A: DANIEL FEARN
Managing director, Stewart Christie

I thought it fitting (and funny) that I should ask my like-minded business partner for his input on a few of the subjects in this chapter. Daniel is the one who made the move to purchase Stewart Christie, which took us on our journey into the world of tailoring and tartan.

Vixy Rae: How did you first know you wanted to be involved in the clothing industry?

Daniel Fearn: I've had a love of clothing from an early age. My grandmother was a regimental seamstress and used to stitch the regalia on to military uniforms to complete them. My mother made a lot of my clothes when I was little, and I always loved getting my clothing allowance when I was a teen, to trawl round the shops and create my own looks. I was the only boy in my school who took textiles as a GCSE, and one of only a few guys to study fashion at university. I loved it; colour and unusual patterns were always lurking in my wardrobe. I was less interested in the industry part and more in the skills and craft of making.

What prompted you to purchase Stewart Christie & Co.?

I've lived in Scotland since the late 1990s and had always worked in clothing and retail. I'd joined the Incorporation of Edinburgh Tailors, one of the city's old trade guilds, and heard that Mr Lowe, the owner of Stewart Christie & Co., was considering retiring and selling the company. You and I had been working together for six years at that point and were both feeling a little disillusioned. The designs we were creating were more mainstream and had Scottish overtones, but the fabric and the manufacturing process of our products were being sourced further and further away from Scotland and the UK.

My passion has always been to create, and Stewart Christie were one of the last companies still designing and creating their products on their own premises. I had helped grow one brand from humble beginnings and I saw Stewart Christie as something which had true heritage. It had survived since 1720 by evolving and creating quality products – and it had reached a point where it needed new life breathed into it. We weren't saving the company – it was profitable – but it was a chance to build on some pretty solid foundations, and

respectfully move it forward for the next generation to enjoy.

What's the first tartan garment you can remember wearing?

This is a sore point, on a few levels. One because it was a bit of a fashion mistake, which I would prefer to forget, and two, I am slightly scarred by it. I must have been about five, and my mother made me a lovely pair of dress Stewart tartan dungarees – which sound pretty cool for the late 1970s, very Bay City Rollers, but they were made from itchy kilt-weight tartan, and were unlined too! I just remember how much they scratched and how I was told, 'Stop making a fuss!' So, when anyone chooses a particularly heavy woollen cloth, I always now ask if they would like their trousers FULLY lined.

Did you know much about Highland dress before coming to Stewart Christie?

To be honest, I only knew the basics, and I felt a complete outsider, not worthy of wearing the garb. It has been a steep learning curve, working out all the outfits and what should be worn on what occasion. It helped massively that Stewart Christie was responsible for putting together the definitive guide to Highland wear, outlining not just the basics but what was correct on state occasions – and the fact it was definitely not okay to wear a bowler hat with a kilt . . .

But that guide was written in 1932, and today just wearing a suit is classed as very formal. What I now find interesting is what can be worn and what is acceptable today. Our next challenge is to define the rules for the next hundred years with a new guide. As trews are becoming more and more popular with younger gentlemen, it's a challenge for us to create the perfect garments to accompany this look – this perhaps means looking back to the 1800s when trews were more popular than kilts. As fashion shifts, we need to be able to keep Highland wear relevant and at the same time abreast of the trends.

What's the most interesting tartan garment you've seen?

There are two levels to this question. From a historical viewpoint it has to be an outfit in the National Museum of Scotland archive. It was created for the royal pageant in 1822. It was a partly bias-cut, three-piece tartan outfit. It was created for a gentleman, and the tartan is not the most subtle – it's orange and green.

The three pieces were: a kilt, a coated doublet and a separate plaid. The jacket is very close-fitting, and the checks are matched amazingly closely for a coat cross-cut. It's the kind of outfit you could wear today – formally – and it wouldn't look out of place. I do love the idea of flamboyance, and the 'peacock male': the pageant was a perfect opportunity for tailors and gentlemen to show their style and creations.

The most interesting contemporary tartan piece has to be the sumptuous cuts from Alexander McQueen's Highland Rape collection. The use of lace, tartan, leather and corsetry is truly feminine and theatrically dramatic at the same time. The black and red of the MacQueen tartan is dark enough to be slightly gothic, and the slender lines and use, again cross-cut, give it an amazingly chic timeless edge. It is something to aspire to in ladies wear – to create something unique but wearable, elegant yet sexy. I think the tartan dress coat you, Vixy, created came close to this. With a close-fitting bodice top and a full-length bias-cut skirt, it's impossibly elegant and still practical, yet something only really to be worn by the clan chief's wife for that dramatic and hierarchical look.

What is your favourite story unearthed from the Stewart Christie archive?

When we purchased Stewart Christie, the archive garments and the old archive books held a massive interest for me. One of the first marketing exercises we undertook was to dust off the archive garments and put together the Masters of Ceremony shoot. The short film and photoshoot was perhaps the best modern story we have done, using old pieces which introduced us as the new owners of the company. It helped show how we were bringing people together, supporting craft, respecting the past, looking at sustainability and still showing the company's legacy. It was a great introduction.

I have since had chance to read through more of the archive and uncover some forgotten stories. My favourite is an interview with Teddy Roosevelt. He stated he had two favourite suits from Scotland, and one had been made by John Christie & Co. (the Christie part of Stewart Christie & Co.). This filled me with pride. As I continued to read, it stated that the suit was not actually his; it had belonged to his grandfather and had been 'handed down' to Teddy. This shows the strength of Stewart Christie was right there in the early days: quality and a timeless elegance. These elements are, I believe, the reason the company is the oldest bespoke tailors left in Scotland . . . built to last and look good for generations!

Do you own any tartan garments?

Shockingly, I don't own any tartan garments, not even a shirt. But I do have several tartan ties, if that counts. There is a good reason for this. I was born in England, but mine is an old Scottish surname. Fearn is an area in the far north of Scotland. There isn't a tartan which I can call my own. I suppose, out of respect for Scottish heritage, I made the conscious decision not to wear a tartan just for the sake of it. I like things to be authentic, so I need to have some connection and relevance to a tartan before I can wear it.

There isn't a 'sept' I can link to. However, my first pair of tartan trews will be in the tri-centennial Stewart Christie tartan and I will wear them with pride. I feel confident of that tartan's story!

So, tartan . . . a cloth to love or to loathe?

Did you ask all your interviewees such open-ended questions or just me? I could answer, 'Yes! I do love it!' But that wouldn't really be very helpful, so I will try and give my best and balanced answer.

I love tartan because it creates pride and unity for a nation which stands apart (not actually) from the rest of the world. For such a small country, Scotland has a global following and tartan is a huge part of that. Tartan is a symbol of belonging and is recognisable the world over. I love the fact that much of tartan's history is shrouded in mystery, the facts are woven together with myth and hidden stories behind each tartan link to the histories of each clan – such a great piece of PR for the country.

On the flipside, I loathe the way tartan is exploited, used to make money and promote a certain image. If tartan is woven and manufactured in Scotland it is special; if it is woven elsewhere it is still tartan, but lacks that authentic back story – and perhaps isn't supporting the Scottish economy. It's hard to rationalise that a cloth can belong to just one nation, but I'm not keen on the fact that it can be used anywhere, without reason or authenticity. The whole point of tartan was that it would have been an honour to wear it, either as part of the family or as part of the clan. Now it is used and abused . . . love the legend, loathe the excess.

REBEL

TARTAN
Sassenach

Rep dark grey
Rep light grey
Rep white
Rep black

This 14th chapter is dedicated to the loving memory of Paul Simon Cuthbertson, 14.12.98.

CUT FROM THE CLOTH

With tartan seeming to be, historically speaking, a male-dominated cloth, I always want to fly the flag for the women in Scotland who strive to create and inspire from their homes in Scotland, those who are at the forefront of the industry and leading the way with their ideas and endeavours. Scotland is a small country, but we certainly punch above our weight when it comes to the sheer volume of creative talent we produce.

As I am – personally and professionally – so deeply involved in fashion and clothing in Scotland it felt great to have an excuse to find and chat to the women featured in this book outside of my professional capacity, so as to understand where their influences and passions hail from. With all our different backgrounds and different dreams, it appears we are cut from the same cloth; we agree on issues which reflect the nation, the people, the future with ideas of sustainability and zero waste echoing throughout all we do.

With the fashion industry being one of the biggest polluters of the planet, a collective consciousness is forming against

the excesses of fast fashion and high-street brands. The focus is shifting towards slow fashion, sustainability and long-lasting style pieces rather than more throwaway trends.

Tartan is what I like to call a generational piece of clothing. The sheer weight of the cloth gives it longevity and, true to the frugal nature of the Scots, it can be handed down to the next generation. These days, more importance is attached to having some authentic provenance to the kilt you wear. Moth holes, repairs and even stains give that certain air of antiquity and are prized as they prove the cloth has been well loved and used; there's a real kudos in wearing a kilt that has enjoyed years of 'active service'.

HERITAGE

With these values in mind, who are the individuals creating the garments that will one day become the heritage pieces of the future? Using the best of the past with ingenuity, creativity and technical advancement, while keeping one eye on the lessons of history and another on the effects upon the future – these are fundamental practices to my bevy of creative beauties.

If there was a new Highland rebellion against fast fashion, Inverness-born Clare Campbell would be leading it. She is the first to admit that her mother has always been the most inspirational person in her life. Yet it was the tragic loss of Clare's brother, Paul, in his late teens that changed her outlook on life, and her family, for ever.

AN INNER REBEL

After this pivotal event, Clare worked hard at her chosen career as an accountant and became a mother herself, to two beautiful children, after marrying her childhood sweetheart. In 2015, her life took a new direction when she found her 'inner rebel' (as she calls it) and discovered something that encompassed all of her passions in one world.

Clare knew she wanted to not only weave and create cloth, but also to build

the mill in which to make her fabric. It was going to be a journey, a long, difficult and perilous journey, but what makes someone a hero is the willingness to be prepared to go above and beyond what is considered 'enough' and push hard for something more. With her sharp tartan and cloth designs, and her robust spirit, Clare started her company Prickly Thistle, thereby taking tartan production back to the Highlands.

Surrounded by her own – and tartan's – heritage, Clare wanted to weave cloth which would push the boundaries of traditional thinking, to encompass a brand of endurance which would tell a tale as interesting as the ones which had inspired her.

When we talk, I am amazed by her passion for tartan, which is so strong that I'm sure, if she were to cut herself, her blood would reveal a tartan pattern running through it. She knows her own mind and is not easily swayed. I get the feeling she has ruffled a few feathers in the world of weaving with her outspokenness, but then she wouldn't be a rebel if she hadn't.

Clare's ambitious three-phase project – the building of a true Highland Mill in an old steading close to her home – is firmly underway. She has gained the funding via Kickstarter and her vision of the Black House Mill is gradually taking shape, along with her passion for bringing education into weaving. By creating authentic cloth with zero waste, she forges forward with a strong set of ideals which, and there can be no doubt about this, she will see through to completion.

THE PRICKLY THISTLE BY CLARE CAMPBELL

People often ask for an introduction, and I always try to make it as interesting and different from the traditional, or the expected. In a nutshell that's what I am – it's the desire to be a bit different – me, Clare, and the vision for Prickly Thistle. Prickly Thistle is not just a tartan brand based in the Highlands of Scotland; it's pitching to be the biggest disruptor in tartan design and textile history. Challenging all of the rules and breaking them, although of course most of them are not actually rules. Being the new rebels on the scene, we don't have a hundred-year history or even a ten-year history. What we do have is generations of passion, innovation and tenacity in our blood.

"The thread counts incorporate Sam Heughan's date of birth – like a vintage dram it is important to know where, when and how it was made.

Q&A: CLARE CAMPBELL
Founder and tartan designer, Prickly Thistle

Vixy Rae: You are passionate about authentic Highland tartan. Your Black House Mill project began in 2017 as a campaign to bring the weaving of tartan back to the Highlands and build the first new mill Scotland has seen in decades. How is this project progressing?

Clare Campbell: There is a complete commitment to regenerating the tartan industry in the region I call home. I have become relentless in making sure it happens. The Black House Mill building project is set to be completed in summer 2020. It will be the only textiles mill ever to be built from the campaign around and the sales of an exclusive tartan collection – the Black House Mill tartan.

What is most exciting about the project is, when this mill building is complete, the sett will be archived and never woven again. All the people from around the world who believed in our vision will be custodians of this specific tartan, each holding a special story-telling cloth, one that's woven by us. I have to disclose, though, that a well-known Scot did give me some extra help in spreading the word!

Where did the name Prickly Thistle come from?

Most may or may not be familiar with the legend of the feisty little weed. Legend has it that the humble thistle secured victory for the Scots in the Battle of Largs in 1263, when the invading Vikings' stealthy approach was ruined when one Norseman stood on a thistle and yelled out in pain. This led to the thistle's appointment as the national flower of Scotland.

On learning this story, I was immediately drawn to the concept of something unexpected having a significant impact – never underestimate the thistle's resilience. Also, as a textiles brand, I wanted people to feel the prickly thistle when they said our name – but I hope not like those unfortunate Norseman!

What core qualities do you want to instil into your cloth and the brand?

It seems I always have a Plan B for everything, and so I have two takes on this. The first is our five 'threads of purpose':

1. To write a new chapter for the story of tartan, one where the Highlands once again plays a pivotal role.

2. To weave innovation into all aspects of what we do. From ensuring the native raw materials of Scotland are once again core to our cloth's construction to developing tartan textile applications that never been seen before.

3. To become custodians of sacred craft skills safeguarding our ancestors' knowledge and sharing this with the next generation.

4. To inject our Highland design flair into every fibre of every project. By creating unique story-telling designs these are translated into the most purposeful product collection imaginable.

5. To ensure that Highland perfection sets an unrivalled standard.

These are the areas we are committed to as we grow the brand, these are our goals. That's one part, but how we do that is equally important and this is backed up by our qualities, the personality traits of the brand, prescribing how we meet our five threads of purpose. These traits are what make us a brand of endurance.

From your background, what or who inspired you to take on this mammoth project?
Life-changing experiences are often catalysts for major change. Losing my younger brother when he was a teenager taught me that life is short – and that's even if you make it to a higher number than him. This took a while to sink in and my life, for over ten years, focused on my family and the family I was yet to have. When I reached

that point, and having worked tirelessly as a chartered accountant, the time came when I could enter my rebel mode, as life really is very, very short.

If you were a tartan what colours would you have and why?
I would only be three colours as three has always been my number. They would be three shades of red: a deep dark blood red, ruby red and traffic-light red. Why? Well, that's for your next book!

I'm sure you've had some interesting collaborations and commissions. Which one has given you as much genuine pleasure as the client?
I think asking the client would be the ultimate validation on this. But yes, recently we were invited to work with what could only be described as the king of a design project for us. Where commitment to Scotland and the belief in all of its undiscovered potential was a key part of the collaboration, plus a healthy dose of rebellious sprit.

Working with Sam Heughan and his personal brand Great Glen Company – which embraces Scottish pride, culture and heritage – has been incredible. Designing a collection of tartan for him, designed and made in the Highlands, has been a personal honour. But most importantly, his support and willingness to work with us has helped me develop even more social and economic benefits under the Prickly Thistle banner. For that we owe him a debt – but

perhaps overcoming the authorities on the question of names makes us equal. Yes, the Sassenach Tartan belongs to Sam, the man who changed the word's definition.

'Sassenach' is a historic Scottish term for all who aren't native to the Gaelic-speaking Highlands. Sam Heughan, a Sassenach himself, was born in Dumfries, lowland Scotland, in 1980. The tartan's threadcount reflects significant dates and times while adopting a subtle black and grey palette. The four colours within the tartan are inspired by Scotland's dark landscape, from rigid natural rock formations to heavy skies rolling in the glens. The thread counts incorporate Sam's date of birth – and, like a vintage dram, it's important to know what year it was made; the Sassenach brand launched in 2019.

With sustainability so important, are you interested in creating fashion or style?
For me it has always been about creating shared values above fashion or style. When you have shared values everything else falls in naturally.

As you take your fresh approach to weaving and creating the cloth, have you encountered much resistance from the establishment?
I like to think we are changing the future by disrupting the past. So, yes, we are plotting a radically fresh approach for the brand over the next few years, and some are curious, shall we say. I'm always very careful to maintain integrity on what

we do and do not do. Therefore, where I felt something was the core business of another Scottish textile-related brand then we didn't do it. Narrowing down the tools in your tool kit makes us more creative with what we have. Less is always more.

Are all tartans beautiful, or are there ones which make you cringe?

The beauty in tartan is in how it makes someone feel, so if a design creates a positive feeling then it's beautiful. Those positive feelings resonate around pride and identity, and today in the global community that we are part of these feelings are the most powerful. I cringe more about what it's woven from and where it's woven than the label!

Were there any mistakes in any of your early designs and creations which turned out to be revelations?

Lots of faux pas and lots of revelations! I don't think that will change and, actually, I don't want it to. Perfection lies in honesty about who you are and what you do, and in the world of design and creation, uniqueness is the DNA of authenticity, so the odd little unplanned moment keeps it real!

PRIDE

TARTAN

Black Watch

Anc green
Anc blue
Black

PAINTINGS OF TARTAN

If we look at historical pieces of art – such as *The Black Watch at Fontenoy, 1745* by William Skeoch Cumming and *The Black Watch at Bay* by W. B. Wollen – it's evident that tartan owes a key aspect of its survival to its military involvement. The historical sett designs of tartan can often be seen in portraiture, but it's sometimes the case that such visions of an individual's identity owe more to artistic flair than to the actual design of the original tartan.

The most famous and accurate of these are the romantic interpretations celebrated in the works of Robert Ranald Mclan of the mid-19th century. His theatrical, heroic warriors sporting kilts and thrusting weapons would surely have set a young lassie's heart a racin' . . . it seems tartan's seductive qualities don't fade over time; well, at least not too much.

ARMED TO THE KILT

Even after the cloth became 'outlawed' in certain types of dress after 1746, there were exceptions. As we have seen, the Act was aimed more at stopping the rough Highlanders from sporting their attire; it didn't extend to women, children and the gentry, nor to parts of the military. The reason as to why some Highland regiments were allowed to retain their kilts, while others were not, feels like a matter of mathematics.

A contemporary analogy might be those signs in the windows of pubs on Easter Road – 'No Football Colours'. Denying the (fighting) men of Highland clans their tartan is a bit like denying hooligans their team's football strip – either way, you've less chance of immediately recognising which side a potential aggressor supports, nor can you gather your own 'tribe' around your cause quite so easily. Disorder and disorientate: that was the rationale.

The Act of Proscription came at a time when the British Empire was rapidly expanding, and more of its soldiers than ever were required to keep the peace and police the far-flung corners of the globe. For the English crown, enlisting the Highland regiments worked on two levels. Firstly, if the British Army could persuade Highlanders to enlist they could count on the skills of some pretty ferocious troops. The flipside was some of Scotland's most troublesome Jacobites could be removed by being relocated – by their own will rather than forcibly. Win-win for the military.

THE DEVIL IN A SKIRT

Dirty, huge and fearless: the reputation of the Scots reached far and wide, and they often hired themselves out as soldiers of fortune. There are historical records of Scots fighting in conflicts through the 1600s in countries such as Norway, Sweden and Germany. Famously, these 'Devils in Skirts' – *Les Diables en Jupes* is a moniker that persisted up to and beyond the First World War – formed two of the most elite fighting forces in France and became the French king's own bodyguards: *les Gardes du Corps*. German troops named them *Die Damen aus der Hölle* – the Ladies from Hell.

A RACY RED

Prior to the Jacobite uprisings, a few lowland regiments used tartan for their uniform. One of which was the King's Own Bodyguard in Scotland. In the early 1700s, the Royal Company of Archers, as they are known, chose a bright red tartan. Some argue this was a deliberate act of rebellion against the Act of Union, but royal portraits show the young Prince George wearing the same cloth. Indeed, a vast array of historical portraits by the likes of Henry Raeburn depict the archers' uniforms in all their glory. In a tradition that continues to this day, positions within the regiment were granted to landed gentry, nobility and prominent local personages – notable individuals with the wealth, power and status to have their portraits painted and admired.

The Royal Company of Archers were, and still are, a ceremonial bodyguard to the reigning monarch. They attend at civic appointments and accompany the monarch. Positions are handed down through the family line, but prowess with an actual bow and arrow is still a requirement – practice shoots and an annual competition are held to test these skills.

The flamboyant uniform might have – fortunately, I would argue – evolved from its original racy red through a deep green tartan, to become the plain rifle green doeskin that was developed during the Victorian revival. You can still see them nowadays: when Queen Elizabeth II attended a public event in Scotland, her resplendent Royal Archers were present.

KEEPING WATCH

As we have seen, tartan's standing is that of a very masculine fabric. And perhaps the most masculine and widely known of all tartans is the Black Watch.

Like many Highland stories, this tale has slightly dubious beginnings. In 1667 Charles II allowed the Earl of Atholl to bring together a company of Highlanders to keep a watch over the 'Braes'. These upland areas were particularly lawless and 'The Watch' were to police them with their broad swords, side pistols and dirks.

But nothing went quite according to plan. The irony being that the Jacobite uprising of 1715 was aided rather than prevented by members of The Watch! This put the not-quite-final nail in the coffin for the regiment, which was disbanded within two years.

SETT IN UNIFORM

This dissolution of the Highland regiments was short-lived, though. They were not forgotten, and the idea was revived in 1725, when six companies were formed; initially these independent companies wore their own clan tartans. The blue and green tartan came later: worn by these companies, it

MUTINY IN THE RANKS

In October 1739 a warrant was signed authorising the raising of four more companies, which would have equated to an extra four hundred men. By late 1739 Black Watch consisted of ten companies, meaning it was at full regimental strength, truly a force to be reckoned with. In May 1740, seven hundred of these men assembled near the bridge over the River Tay in Aberfeldy. Under the control of the Earl of Crawford, the Colonel of the new regiment, Black Watch was granted the number of the 43rd Regiment.

Then, in July 1742, a decision was made to march the Regiment south, ostensibly to be inspected by King George II, but he had already sailed to Europe. However, in May 1743 they were inspected on Finchley Common by Major General Wade, with many thousands of spectators watching. Rumours were rife that they were to be shipped to the West Indies; hardly the most enticing of postings, especially when you'd signed up to serve in Scotland. And so, one evening a group of one hundred soldiers decided to head home – an act the powers-that-be saw as mutiny. Surrounded in a wood seventy miles away from London, the mutineers were marched to the Tower of London. Many of them spoke only their native Gaelic, but all were found guilty. The three ringleaders were shot; the others dispatched to the colonies in America. Not the most glorious start for the Regiment, but their bravery at the Battle of Fontenoy in May 1745 earned them the name of the Highland Furies.

was instantly recognisable throughout the 18th century and was commonly known as the government tartan. But Major General Wade had the clever idea to create different variants of the same tartan for different companies. It was a simple matter to keep the same base but introduce other colours as overchecks. This stroke of historical genius enabled the tartan to be still recognisable as it evolved to the darker-hued fabric we know today. As a basis Black Watch was a perfect sett and colour, but with the nuance of subtle differences in the overchecks, the regimental tartans were born.

pour the blast of death. I come abroad on the winds: the tempests are before my face. But my dwelling is calm, above the clouds; the fields of my rest are pleasant.

Rousing stuff indeed! Words such as these helped cement Gaelic heroes in literary history, building on their image as romantic warriors roaming across the sweeping Highlands. But, like tartan, the origins of the Poems of Ossian are up for debate: stolen, reworked and retold . . . it would appear that James Macpherson might have some explaining to do.

TWO GENTLEMEN OF THE BLACK WATCH

A visit to Balhousie Castle made my Black Watch research significantly more straightforward. It's home to the Black Watch Museum and the place where I met two gentleman who are founts of knowledge on the regiment, the tartan and its glorious history. Lt Col. (Retd) Roddy Riddell and Maj. (Retd) Ronnie Proctor have both served in the regiment since the early 1970s, and their passion for the Watch is contagious.

FOR THE LACK OF CLOTH

The regiment has been involved in all conflicts near and far since its formation, with notable presence in the Boer War, the Napoleonic wars and the American War of Independence. However, it was a period in the early 20th century that held more interest for me in relation to the cloth and some little-

WARRIOR POETS

Despite such setbacks, the Highland regiments were always there to lead the charge. But during the Napoleonic Wars of the early 19th century, there was a shortage of true Scots to fill their kilted regiments and so the Irish and English were recruited to swell its ranks. Whether they wore the tartan of the Black Watch with splendid ferocity is unrecorded, although James Macpherson's 'Ossian' poems of the 1860s would have us believe that the sight of the Scots regiments struck fear into the hearts of their enemies:

The people bend before me. I turn the battle in the field of the brave. I look on the nations, and they vanish: my nostrils

known historical facts. One fact was that during the First World War the 42nd Battalion Royal Highlanders of Canada (Black Watch) ran out of tartan for their kilts, and the decision was made to make the kilts in the Black Watch tweed instead. The tweed had a stronger, hardier look and a tone more akin to the battle dress of the English troops with their khaki tunics and overalls.

BATTLE DRESS

The kilt in the Black Watch archive has the traditional 'pleat to stripe', but the box pleats have 'barrelled' pleats in the top. This barrelled effect was created by inserting a cane up into the top of the pleat and then pressing over the top to give a curved appearance. The barrel look is particular to this time; later a 'knife' pleat was favoured as it gave a sharper finish, is easier to achieve and more likely to stay in place.

GAS PANTS

The Great War saw huge changes in combat with the advent of the machine gun, and the use of mustard gas as a new and horrific weapon. Before the introduction of gas masks, the Black Watch were instructed to remove their hose, pee on them, then interlock and wrap them around their nose and mouth area to prevent inhalation of the gas. This 'safety measure' caused problems of its own as the gas

simply crept up and under the kilt, causing significant discomfort to the soldiers' unprotected nether regions. This in turn led to the creation of 'gas pants', which the soldiers wore to stop the mustard gas 'invading the lowland regions'.

THE BLACK WATCH ARCHIVE

As with all tartan, the main changes for Black Watch have been in texture, weight and colour. But Black Watch's bold and distinctive strength means it has certainly stood the test of time. Its deep navy and bottle-green tones are perhaps the best known and most widely used of all tartans. When I explored the kilts in the Black Watch archive, which date from 1830 onwards, the style remains steady, but differences in yarn, dye and weave are easy to spot.

My journey to Perth to meet with Ronnie and Roddy, heroes both, taught me so much about the legendary Black Watch regiment and the secrets of its tartan.

Q&A: RODDY RIDDELL AND RONNIE PROCTOR
The Black Watch Museum

Vixy Rae: Black Watch appears to be the oldest tartan in continuous use. How old is it?

Roddy Riddell: It can be officially dated back to 1739/40.

Would Black Watch tartan and Black Watch tweed ever have been worn together?

RR: No, they would not have been worn together. The first tweed was made prior to the Great War and was worn by officers as a country suit or for shooting.

The Black Watch tartan was originally purple and blue, then evolved over time. Were the original colours from a particular region or from the dyes that were readily available?

Ronnie Proctor: My take is that, like many things, cost would have been a factor, as would where and when the tartan was woven; these would lead to subtle variants. More can be discovered in *The Black Watch Tartan: An Examination and Assessment of the Work of H. D. Macwilliam* by James D. Scarlett (2005)!

Who was the most influential colonel when it came to the uniform? And how did his regime change things for the regiment?

RR: It was the change in warfare that forced the change in uniform. During the Boer War the jackets worn were khaki, with aprons which were worn to protect the kilt. Then at the start of the Second World War, Highland soldiers wore battledress and the kilt was withdrawn.

RP: Colonel Duncan Cameron, who commanded the 42 from 1843 onwards, was instrumental in regulating the dress in the regiment. He commanded the 42 during the Crimean War where, owing to the extremes of weather – very hot summers and almost arctic winters – different forms of dress set in.

I'm intrigued by the Black Watch Mutineers. Can you tell me who they were?

RP & RR: About two hundred men refused to take foreign service, and marched in the direction of their northern homes. After a parley when in Northamptonshire, they laid down their arms and returned to the Tower of London where they were court marshalled. Three (Farquhar Shaw, and Malcolm and Samuel MacPherson) were deemed to be the leaders and were shot on Tower Hill. The others were transferred to other regiments and sent to various destinations abroad.

Do you know how many variants of the Black Watch there have been? Have you heard of the Brown Watch tartan?
RR: The patterns existent in the early 21st century were the Government No. 1 (Black Watch) and No. 1A (Argyll & Sutherland Highlanders). I have never heard of the Brown Watch tartan!

RP: I have seen the Brown Watch – otherwise known as the 'ancient' or 'muted' Black Watch tartan – which has come into being over recent years. It is normally used by kilt-hire firms for weddings and dress hire. There is also a 'dress' variety with white in it, which was worn as a competition tartan by the Pipes and Drums of 51st Highland Volunteers, and which was later titled the 3rd Battalion Black Watch. This was for civilian use only.

VR: My understanding is that Brown Watch was a request made by an American to a tartan mill in Scotland. At first the mill laughed – and then, being Scots, they shrugged, wove a Brown Watch variant and sold it!

The museum has some truly amazing pieces. Which piece of clothing holds the most poignant story for you?
RR: It has to be the kilt worn by Captain William Stewart of Ardvorlich when he was killed during the Battle of the Somme on 25 September 1916.

RP: I agree. There's also the Glengarry Cap Badge with a German sniper's bullet hole almost through the centre of the badge.

Where is the home of the Black Watch?
RR: For many years it was the now demolished Queen's Barracks in Perth which was our Regimental Depot, but since the early 1960s it has been Balhousie Castle in Perth. The Regimental Museum is housed in the castle.

Much of the uniform looked ornate but had a very practical purpose. Can you explain a few of the details and their functions?

RP: The officer's sash, which is coloured deep red, was worn by non-kilted regiments around the waist. The Black Watch and subsequent Highland regiments took to wearing it over the right shoulder. The purpose of this was:

1. To signify rank.
2. To act as a bandage to cover the wound of a wounded officer and hide the flow of blood from the men.
3. To act as a stretcher to carry a wounded officer from the field.

Heavy gilt-embroidered shoulder boards not only showed the officer's rank but also gave a degree of protection to the shoulders from sword cuts, particularly cavalry sabres.

Did the regiment always wear kilts? Or do trews make an appearance in its history?
RP: Trews were worn in the regiment for the same reason that they were worn by civilians – that is, by those who were mounted. Wearing a philibeg or small kilt was not a practical proposition on horseback. However, during the Napoleonic period, white or blue pantaloons were worn, with tartan trews being worn by the 1840s. Soldiers wore tartan trews for fatigues (work parties), musketry drill, off duty in barracks and for walking out. The Queen's Own Cameron Highlanders, Seaforth Highlanders and the Gordon Highlanders all wore trews more often than the Black Watch and the Argyll and Sutherland Highlanders.

It should be noted that the philibeg began life as part of the belted plaid (the 12-yard belted plaid), and after wear and tear in the campaigns of the north the order was given to reduce the belted plaids to the philibeg for wearing off duty in the evening in barracks.

DISTRICT

TARTAN
Hawick

Rep gold
Anc white
Anc blue
Rep red
Anc green

FORAGING FOR COLOUR

There are two very different ways to look at what is called the 'district' tartan. Firstly, back in the mists of time, cloth woven in a particular location was bound to the colours which could be created from those natural elements that could be foraged. These would have depended on the season and abundance of the plants and so on used for the dye. We have explored the simple truth that tweed transitioned into tartan as weaving techniques became more complex along with yarn and equipment – and, likewise, the technology of dye impacts the look of tartans from particular districts.

Thus, the district tartan was a clear forerunner for the clan tartan; with weavers having the skill and technique, the 'customer' was bound to their styling and knowledge . . . until perhaps that one customer wanted 'something different'.

This would usually have been the clan chief stamping his authority and his desire to be recognised. With these demands, the cloth begins to evolve. Perhaps it holds the same regional colours, but the look of it becomes more to do with the sett design.

ALLEGIANCES MADE AND BROKEN

However, there is also a second view of the district tartan. This holds that after the official registration of tartan and the renaissance of the cloth, which saw it become the height of fashion, there were still perhaps only around fifty tartans. In a shrewd move by the mills, the 'district' tartan was developed as a way of boosting potential sales. This saw the number of tartans climb to around 250. It's an approach to tartan that was particularly effective in lowland areas where the population wanted to be recognised wearing a 'symbol of their nation' without such symbols showing an association to any particular family.

Either way, the wearing of a district tartan isn't really a sign of rebellion. Rather it shows a sense of belonging, a feeling of unity and connection to a particular locale. There's something of an irony, then, in the fact that, as the district tartans fell away, they were actually adopted by the clans of the area. An irony that's all very confusing as we untangle the threads of this story – the clan names were often taken from the land, so there would be a natural evolution of signifiers from district to clan.

If we look at districts and clans together, it's very noticeable that the vast majority of older clan tartans from the west coast and west Highland areas have very similar colouration. If you look at the MacDonald tartan and the MacLeod from Skye, they have a dominance of blue, blue and green; whereas if you travel inland and north to the domains of the Chisholms, the Grants and MacDonnells you will see that the base of their tartans are a bright red with the deep green becoming the secondary colour.

With clans invading, warring and taking control of neighbouring lands, these confrontational activities were, unsurprisingly, seen as exerting a form of control and conformity over the conquered locals. But in trying to unpick the outcomes of these shifts in identity and belonging, it seems any rules and laws of where and why are blended with folklore and myth, adding a beguiling sense of mystery and secrecy to it all. As tartan is shared, borrowed and adapted, so the complex mystique of the noble cloth deepens.

FROM ECOSSE TO KERNOW

Having said all that, there's a slightly more dishonest and commercially driven reason for some of the district cloths. I'm sure they won't mind me divulging, but it's the fabled mill of William Wilson of Bannockburn that is responsible for this. It's recorded that in 1819 some of their 'miscellaneous' patterns were cunningly given English names to boost their appeal to those families south of the border who wanted to share in the look 'Ecosse'. This is where we find the Durham tartan, Cornish, Devon, Plymouth, Carlisle and Yorkshire tartans. To my eye, it would appear that – just as with whisky – Scotland keeps the best of its famous exports for its own consumption. Either that or those

crafty Bannockburn designers and weavers simply wanted the English to stand out a mile when wearing the cloth, my case in point being the Cornish tartan.

THE HAWICK TARTAN

In the midst of these rather hazy myths, it is refreshing to find a story of tartan's provenance that's both truthful and real. This tale of one particular district tartan is close both in time and to my heart. It was back in the early 1990s – not the 1890s – that the cloth was created. The tartan in question is the Hawick tartan. It was the inspiration of one man, Robin Deas, along with the help of Andrew Elliot, a Selkirk mill owner, and their friend Ken Hood.

In the 1990s the future of Hawick – a town about thirty miles south of Edinburgh – was by no means certain. The town had enjoyed a productive and lucrative past that saw it famed the world over for its knitwear and weaving. However, by the start of the 1990s, competition from abroad was having a significant, negative impact on sales of the town's exports to both domestic and international markets.

In these difficult times, one man, Robin Deas – then working in Hawick for one of the large garment producers – had the idea to create a cloth that would bring a sense of unity to his troubled community. Having researched local history for inspiration and colour reference, the initial designs were whittled down to what was still a baffling 27 different drawings. Ken Hood was the brains behind the digitisation of the

designs, not such a straightforward task as it might sound, given this was when computer-aided design was very much in its infancy.

Even so, when all the designs were completed, Robin and Ken sat down with their friend Andrew Elliot to ask for his opinion and advice. Robin started flicking through the designs, then came to a sudden stop. When asked what he was looking at, he simply replied, 'The Hawick Tartan.' Within three days Andrew had it on the looms at his mill: the first piece of the Hawick tartan was in production.

WOVEN IN HAWICK

The woven cloth was then presented to the civic leaders of the town and, after a series of confidential meetings, it was agreed that the tartan should be registered and become the town of Hawick's official tartan. Today the cloth is woven in small quantities and is a particular favourite of those living in and around Hawick. At Stewart Christie, we

have been commissioned to make trews, kilts and skirts in the Hawick tartan, and there are plans to create product ranges including scarves and ties in the near future.

The truth is that, sadly, the processes, thinking and imagination which lie behind many of Scotland's tartans have been lost. And so, the provenance of the Hawick tartan is one of those lovely stories which needs to be recorded and celebrated, drawing the cloth into its rightful place in Scotland's history.

I am not so naive to think that this cloth has the potential to take international catwalks by storm, but it continues to have the potential to bring a community together and celebrate the achievements of the few and the many. This power is a side of tartan I really do love; it's the human side, the truth behind the romance.

AN APPRECIATION OF THE HAWICK DESIGN

Now, more than two decades after its creation, there are a few variants of the Hawick cloth, but the original design incorporates a significant list of colours. **Royal blue and gold** are taken from the pennant of the Priory of Hexham, captured by Hawick's Youths at Hornshole in 1514 and borne each year by the Cornet at the Common Riding. The Common Riding is itself something of a wonder! It's a Borders equestrian festival held annually to uphold the celebrations of the 13th and 15th centuries. People come from far and wide to see male riders parade and race through the town.

Field green and white appear to refer to the Hawick Rugby team.

Navy blue and white are the colours of the Hawick High School.

Dark green is taken from the Douglas tartan with its historical link to Drumlanrig Tower. The 16th-century three-storey towerhouse is now the Borders Textile Towerhouse, a modern museum that celebrates two hundred years of textile history in Hawick.

Red running through the tartan represents the blood spilled by the men of Hawick – on the battlefields of Flodden in 1513 and, over the centuries, on battlefields around the world.

A FUTURE FOR DISTRICT TARTANS

The story of Hawick is so free from pretension, so imbued with a sense of friendship and community, that it's hard not to feel a genuine pride in the cloth. As a tailor, I have used the dress version for a number of ladies' garments; there is something noble and distinct about it.

When I spoke with Robin Deas, it was a joy to hear the passion he still has for the design and how it is still sold (in small quantities) the world over thanks to

the internet and far-flung people chasing connections to their genealogy.

Although some may view it as folly, these tartan lives do have long and far-reaching effects. For what is history if we are not creating it now for the next generation to use and muse over? So perhaps a district tartan is something more Scottish towns should do? Could their towns be celebrated in a cloth that gives a regional identity and recognised focus for historical events . . .

True, the cynic might see it as meaningless tourist fodder – and, if seen from a distance, I would agree. But when you get close enough to hear the stories, to meet the people behind it all, to touch, cut and shape the fabric involved, there is something heart-stoppingly real and honest about the act of using cloth to create unity.

Q&A: ROBIN DEAS
Owner, the Hawick Tartan Company

Vixy Rae: Can you tell me about your connection with Hawick, and your career?

Robin Deas: I was born in 1942 in the Haig Maternity Hospital, and my father was the bank manager of the British Linen Bank in Melrose and Lanark. In 1957 I joined Braemar Knitwear Ltd; my family had big interests in the company, making it natural that I followed that path. In the early 1960s I qualified as a textile technician, then went to London – spending six months at Harrods where I met heads of state, royals and film stars: an unforgettable time. Later, after a spell at Kinloch Anderson in the 1970s I brought my family back to the place

I love, Hawick!

How would you describe yourself, both personally and career wise?

I am a very creative person and, with my technical experience, have been able to maximise my love of product and marketing. Meeting people in many countries, bringing to Hawick many millions of pounds worth of orders and giving people opportunities has been a real joy.

What was your inspiration behind creating the Hawick tartan? I would love to hear it in your own words.

The Hawick tartan came from a feeling that the town needed something to give it a boost. Knitwear and tweeds used to be its main products. By giving the town a strong colourful tartan, highlighting its proud achievements, I hoped to inspire others to help the town and its future.

What impact do you think this had on the town, and are you exploring other variants?

The original launch was fantastic. However, unfortunate circumstances allowed it to slip into the background. The re-launch in 2017 with James Sugden was a fresh start. James and I had many ideas for the tartan; besides making it a viable product and bringing forward the ANC, Weathered and Dress varieties, we also wanted part of the profits to go to selected charities. The local talent that has produced such diverse Hawick Tartan products has been awesome.

Where has the vast majority of cloth been sold, locally or internationally?
Most of the material made has been used locally, but perhaps a third of everything made has gone abroad to those who enjoy the tartan's colours and history.

What are your fondest memories of the time when you created the cloth?
There are many wonderful moments in the tartan's life. The best moment must be when I handed Andrew Elliot my paper designs. I wish I had filmed his face when he found the tartan from the 20-odd pages. He knew immediately that it was the one.

What products have you created from the cloth? And have they been made locally?
All items have been made in the Scottish Borders by a wide range of companies.

I'm particularly fond of the Hawick Tartan teddy bear, Teri, and our special edition of twenty Common Riding bears.

Do you think the mantle will be handed on to the next generation to carry forward?
I have retired from front-line manufacturing, but my love of the industry carries on. I get so much satisfaction from creating things others might enjoy, and while I do so, I will potter on.

With the trend for tweed in tartan patterns, will we see this translation appear on the dapper riders of the Annual Hawick Common Riding soon?
When we first introduced the Hawick tartan, many thought it would become part of the Common Riding dress, if only as a waistcoat. The traditional clothing of tweed jackets won't change. I'm happy the Hawick hasn't been heavily involved; it might have been too much.

With today's focus on local and sustainable cloth, do you think Hawick might regain some of its lost mills and manufacturing?
You ask the impossible. I have watched the industry from the 1940s where knitwear, tweed and spinning in Hawick employed around 12,000 people each day – they'd come into town on the trains and buses. Today, we probably employ some 2,000, but technology plays a big part. It's sad so many of the famous brands have gone, but we fight on and the industry today is versatile, creative and at the top of the quality spectrum.

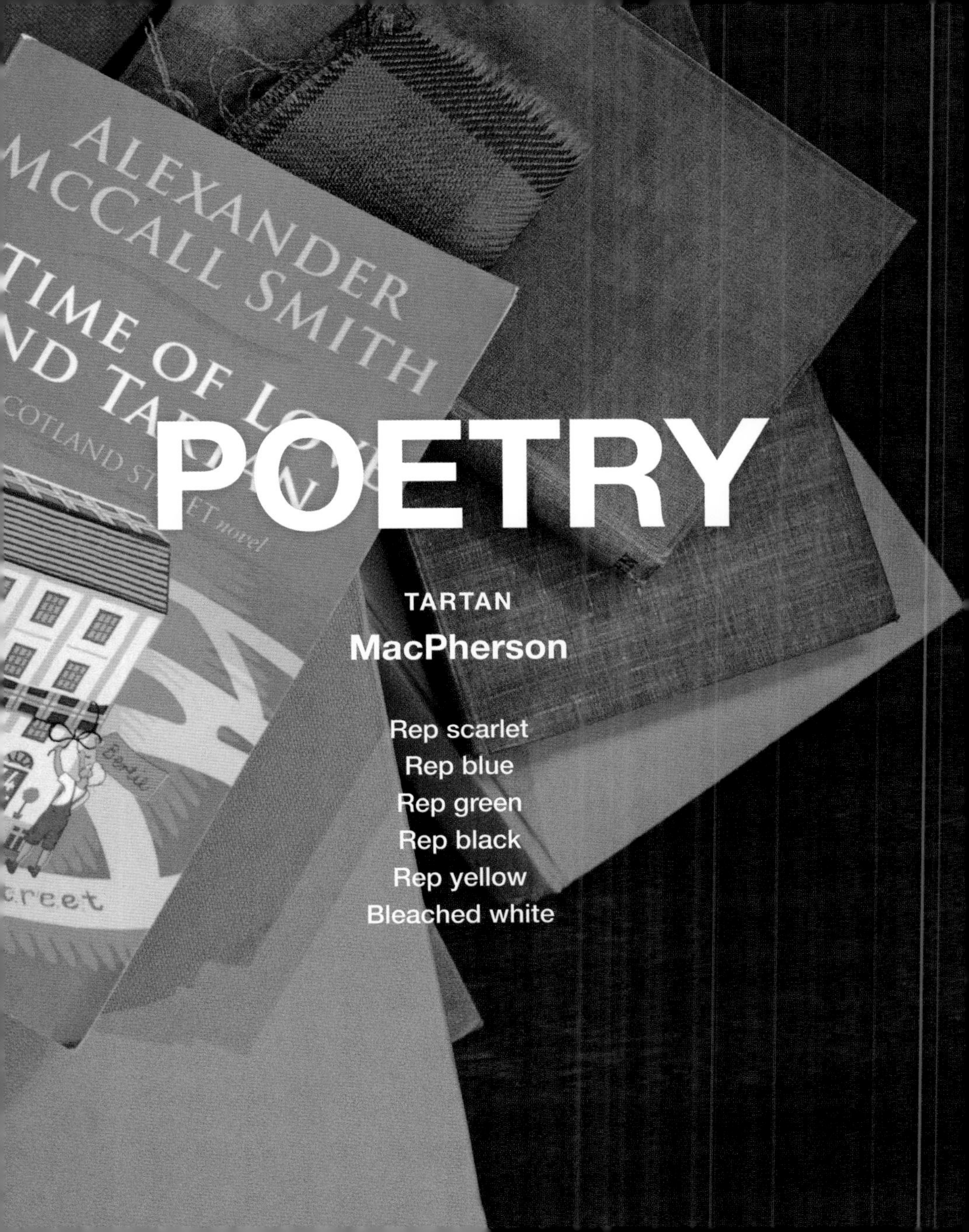

POETRY

TARTAN
MacPherson

Rep scarlet
Rep blue
Rep green
Rep black
Rep yellow
Bleached white

AUNT JULIA HAS THE SPIN

'Words placed in the best order': that is how poetry was always described to me. I was blessed in that my step-grandfather, Norman MacCaig OBE, who some consider a 'poet's poet', gave me a firm grounding in the creation of poetry. For me personally, poetry is like a mesmerising spell or an incantation; it can transport the reader back in time, transcend distance and capture a sense of place, a sense of belonging. It conveys strong emotion in a direct and charming way.

Aunt Julia spoke Gaelic
very loud and very fast.
I could not answer her –
I could not understand her.

She wore men's boots
when she wore any.
– I can see her strong foot,
stained with peat,
paddling with the treadle of the spinning
*   wheel*
while her right hand drew yarn
marvellously out of the air.

A CALL TO ARMS

In Jacobite poetry, Gaelic was often used to give the verses a deeper connection to the Highlands. Like most traditional poetry, it was composed to be chanted or sung aloud – in this case, a rallying cry for the Jacobite cause. The written word also brought the glory of tartan to life in this period, initiating a tradition that would be continued by the likes of Sir Walter Scott for years afterwards. Single words such as 'breacan' – the belted Plaid – and 'èileadh', which meant folded, were worked into the poetry along with 'fèileadh-beag' or 'philibeg' which became the short kilt as we know it today.

> The Highland hearts are living yet,
> As noble as before:
> But where are now the Highland garb,
> The pibrochd, the claymore,
> The philabeg, the cotagarr,
> And all the fair array,
> That cheer'd the friend, and scar'd the
> foe—
> O tell me, where are they . . .

The above is taken from 'The Highland Garb', written for the first grand anniversary meeting of The Highland Garb Society, which took place in the Ossianic Hall, in winter 1839. The banquet was attended by several hundred Highlanders, all attired in their national garb.

THE CLANRANALD BARD

Perhaps the most famous Jacobite poet was Alasdair mac Mhaighstir Alasdair / Alexander MacDonald, the 'Clanranald bard', who composed stirring and rousing verse for the cause. A Gaelic teacher and Jacobite officer who fought in the Battle of Culloden, his work ushered in a new age for Gaelic poetry. His one collection of poems, *Aiseirigh na Seann Chànain Albannach*, published in 1751, was the first Gaelic poetry book ever to be printed.

His work is less well known than Rabbie Burns', but many scholars believe it's just as important. Perhaps his political views are why his work wasn't treated with the

respect it deserved. His words are stirring and powerful in this excerpt from 'The Storm' translated into English:

The sea all lifts up, like a great black coat,
rising to cover the sky, like a shroud,
thrown out,
soaring up, like a blanket, coarse
stuff, shaggy its surface, a big horse's pelt
in black winter,
a cataract rising, a waterfall soaring,
returning itself to its source,
unnatural, screaming and screeching and
howling and yowling,
and ocean becomes: mountains and bens
and valleys and glens,
all rough with the forest and bushes and
grass.
Sea opens its mouth, is all mouth, all
agape,
widening, opening, sharpened the teeth, all
crocodile-strong, hippopotamus tusks, and
gripping and turning,
as if wrestling was fun, forcing over each
one –
Sky shrinks and clenches long ribs on its
brow –

It has turned to ferocity now –
The fight to the death has begun.

Alexander's poem *An Airce* ('The Ark') – a criticism and satire of the members of Clan Campbell who fought against the Jacobites – caused him to flee Edinburgh in 1751, where he had eventually settled after Culloden, back to the Highlands. His 'outrageous' poetry was reportedly seized by the authorities and burned at the Mercat Cross on Edinburgh's High Street. In the poem he promises that the Campbell Clan will be plagued and scourged for their treason against Scotland, while he himself will build a ship of refuge for those Campbells true to the Jacobite cause. All those who seek his shelter, swallow the sea salt water of purgatory and are willing to reject allegiance to the British crown. They didn't catch them all, though – and even now there are a dozen original copies left in existence. It's incredible to think how poetry could quite literally ignite such passion.

FRAGMENTS OF POETRY

This chapter celebrates the MacPherson tartan, so here is James Macpherson, not the only bard to don the MacPherson clan tartan.

James Macpherson was the first Scottish poet to achieve international recognition. Born and raised in Inverness-shire in the 1730 and 1740s, he is best known for his translation of the Ossian cycle of epic poems which had previously only existed in oral form.

In 1760, James published *Fragments of Ancient Poetry Collected in the Highlands of Scotland*, a book so popular among the literary circles of the time that he was commissioned to scour the land looking for other forgotten texts and seeking out oral poetry. From 1760 onwards he published a number of poems from the Ossian cycle, which he claimed had originally been composed by the third-century bard, Ossian. Recording these stories helped to preserve an important part of the Highland culture which might, perhaps, otherwise be lost as the Jacobite rebellion was crushed and the clan structures torn apart.

Though the authenticity of the Ossian poems was questioned – modern-day scholars now agree that Macpherson wrote the poems himself, basing them on old folk tales from the Highlands – they caught the mood of the moment. It is rumoured that Lord Byron was inspired to write *Childe Harold's Pilgrimage*, his own epic, after reading Ossian, and it is recorded that Napoleon travelled with a copy of Macpherson's book on his person.

The poets of the 18th century were the rock stars of their age. They were fêted in society, had an irresistible glamour about them, and, as their works were circulated and sold nationwide, it was the height of

fashion to be in possession of the latest release of the voice of the moment.

NOT QUITE THE LAST MINSTREL

The most prominent Scottish voice of his era was Sir Walter Scott. Edinburgh-born, he started writing poetry in 1805 – his first success was 'The Lay of the Last Minstrel' – and continued in a similar vein until being inspired, somewhat ironically, by Lord Byron to write a novel.

Scott's first novel was the romantic bestseller *Waverley* (named after the Edinburgh train station, or is it the other way around?). He first published it under another name, fearing it would tarnish his reputation and disgrace his legal career. The protagonist of the tale, Edward Waverley, is a young English solider who comes from a Hanoverian background. On joining the army, just before the Jacobite uprising of 1745, he learns he has an uncle with Jacobite sympathies. Edward's loyalties are called into question when he finds himself allied to both the English and Jacobite causes, while falling in love with a Jacobite woman. It's a classic – though rather unwieldy – novel that effectively sums up the recurring themes of division within a nation and the identity crisis which defined Scotland in the 18th century.

Waverley can be seen as the forerunner of the period drama, and it shows Scott's romantic view of the past and Scottish culture. He was also a realist and sought to promote the union of Scotland and England, hence the great Pageant of 1822.

A SELECTION OF BOOKISH TARTANS

Scott's novels were so popular that Wilsons of Bannockburn were enthused to produce a number of tartans using his characters' names. They created a Rob Roy tartan, from *Ivanhoe*, they created a Merrilees tartan and they even produced a Wellington and Waterloo tartan inspired by Scott's 1816 poem, 'The Field of Waterloo'. Naturally, Wilsons sold a Sir Walter Scott tartan too. It no doubt sounds a little money-grabbing, but Wilsons would gladly name a pattern after anything that helped tartan sell. Sir Walter Scott and Wilsons together formed a strong part of 'Brand Scotland'.

Two years after the pageant Scott wrote a novel focusing on the fiction of a third uprising where Bonnie Prince Charlie returned to lead the struggle. *Redgauntlet* again indicates Scott's inner struggle – who should rule, his head, his creditors or his heart?

A GIFT FOR WORDS

Amid all these masculine voices was Alice MacDonell of Keppoch. She was born in 1854 and her great-great-grandfather had led the MacDonalds at Culloden. She, like Macpherson, rediscovered the passions of the Rising. One of her poems directly refers to tartan, using the cloth as a symbol and metaphor for the threads which bind the Scots together.

ALICE MACDONELL
'The Weaving of the Tartan'

I saw an old Dame weaving,
Weaving, weaving
I saw an old Dame weaving,
A web of tartan fine.
'Sing high,' she said, 'sing low,' she said,
'Wild torrent to the sea,
That saw my exiled bairnies torn,
In sorrow far frae me.
And warp well the long threads,
The bright threads, the strong threads;
Woof well the cross threads,
To make the colours shine.'
She wove in red for every deed,
Of valour done for Scotia's need:
She wove in green, the laurel's sheen,
In memory of her glorious dead.
She spake of Alma's steep incline,
The desert march, the 'thin red line',
Of how it fired the blood and stirred the heart,
Where'er a bairn of hers took part.
''Tis for the gallant lads,' she said,
'Who wear the kilt and tartan plaid:
'Tis for the winsome lasses too,
Just like my dainty bells of blue.
So weave well the bright threads,
The red threads, the green threads;
Woof well the strong threads
That bind their hearts to mine . . .'

Their hearts a kindly glow.
So weave well the bright threads,
The red threads, the green threads.
Woof well the strong threads
That bind their hearts to thine.

To me, Alice's work is a simple, classic poem, a snapshot in time. Published in 1894, it was perhaps written earlier. Alice ended her days in Hove, on England's south coast, but the MacDonells of Keppoch can be traced to the 14th century when they were granted the Isle of Lewis by David II. Those were the days! Although I would have preferred a gift of Harris myself . . .

TARTAN IN POETIC FORMS

In these more troubled modern times, it is often wise to seek counsel from a balanced and considered individual. For me, such a person is the admirable, utterly gracious Alexander McCall Smith, who was kind enough to offer me his words, in their best order, to embody a modern view on the traditional, cultured cloth.

Alexander McCall Smith has been an avid supporter of Stewart Christie & Co., having mentioned the company a few times in his Scotland Street novels. I have long admired his writing's fluid and relaxed form, how he always captures those small passing thoughts and details which give his characters such depth. It is indeed Alexander McCall Smith who is the significant other, an advocate of the MacPherson tartan.

I can't think of a more beautiful way to finish this chapter than with these gorgeous lines of poetry by Sandy (as I'm lucky enough to call him). They capture the magic and energy of tartan perfectly. A notion travelling through different spaces and landscapes, giving the cloth context though fantasy and memory mixed with pride and belonging.

ALEXANDER McCALL SMITH
'THE IDEA OF TARTAN'

1. A dream

My dearest, last night it was in a dream
That I stood outside a window, and within
Saw the dancers lined, prepared
For one of those reels that require
A moment of contemplation before
The dance begins; I was not excluded,
But had gone outside for air,
To watch, with lawn underfoot,
And feel the gentle touch of night,
For it was summer in my dream
And it was warm. Music drifted out
And the dance began;
The ordered rows of dancers,
Experts each, paid the courtesies
That such occasions require,
Their kilts and skirts, their sashes,
Were splashes of colour
Against the white walls of a village hall,

Reds, blues, greens, they were
A pulsating artery of colour,
And drabness, and silence,
Were absent from that dance,
Uninvited to that party.
The pulse of the music
Was the beat of a country's heart,
Something precious, something glimpsed
That survives the watered-down, the
    inauthentic,
The substitute for love and feeling;
Fortunate that dream, and happy its vision
Vouchsafed me before dawn
And the awakening it brought;
I felt myself specially blessed
To have seen what I really could not see –
To have been embraced
By the colours of belonging.

2. In Sicily

In Sicily the Highlanders
Brought liberation mile by mile,
The Fifty-First Division
Found quarters in the places
Where occupation had silenced
The gentler sounds of a southern landscape,
The screech of cicadas, the bel canto;
And now the young piper is
In his kilt, the tartan green
Against the parched browns
Of the Mezzogiorno *across the straits;*
The white of dust hangs in the air;
The pale blue creates a cloudless sky;
He plays Farewell to the Creeks,
And each phrase of the music
Breaks the heart, breaks the heart.

3. Remember me

Remember me, as I remember you,
That June, on an island,
With Ben Mhor somewhere distant,
Somewhere blue, and the slow
Passage of the sea with its tides,
And you wearing the colours
That to me are the colours
Of the land, and of you;
And the wind from Coll, from Tiree,
Whispering to us: Do not be afraid,
Do not be afraid to love one another;
Do not be afraid to love a land.

DESIGN

TARTAN
Campbell

Rep green
Rep blue
Rep black

UNCONVENTIONALITY

My career has taken an unconventional path. A journey from streetwear to traditional tailoring is not a natural progression and I do feel I've had to grow up slightly to hold my own in the traditional milieu, though I'd like to think I've done that in a way that's graceful and stays true to who I am. My core values from an early age have always been unconventional and my tastes have always been more eclectic than clothing that's corporate and mass produced.

The true genus of my designs has always stayed focused around clean lines, subtle design detailing and authentic quality; from sneakers to brogues, I have always enjoyed a touch of 'the check' but avoided the full throttle of mainstream tartan. There are those who can, and I do appreciate it, look stunning in 'full tartan' but, for me, it has always been about incorporating it into the subtle details of an outfit – where you perhaps have to look twice to notice the tartan rather than it shouting at you to pay attention.

My heart has always been steeped in colour, yet I find myself dressing mostly these days in black or grey. Delving deeper into the depths of tartan, I have reignited a lost love, realising that the colours can be more refined and less 'sudden'. For example, the muted hues from the weathered reiver tartan give a faded tone to the cloth. I suppose this is the reason I love tweed so much but don't always reach for it first in the wardrobe; it's not my instinctive style, but I do appreciate the depth of colour in the yarn and the nature of the weave.

With my love of design and my wee Scottish roots, I am most inspired when designing collections that have an elegant nod to history. Less is more in my mind, yet I am led by my customers when it comes to bespoke garments. Clients appreciate my approach and style, but at the same time they like to put their own personal stamp on garments, and this usually starts with the fabric. My true passion in life is for people, and I feel blessed to work with so many different personalities to create individual pieces, all with their own character and stories.

Style can be timeless, whereas fashion is present in the moment. Combining these two elements gives a garment longevity, making it less disposable and less likely to date. If in doubt, I look to classic pieces to see what inspires me, then I take it from there. Remodel, repair and repurpose are the three Rs I advocate when making clothes; by creating timeless pieces in quality fabrics, my aim is to combine all three.

It does take courage to wear colour, and it can often seem that the palette of the modern age tends to be more toned down. This is why I have selected four incredible women to highlight here. They inspire me so much, from weaving tartan, to dressmaking, stunning couture and super styling through modelling, all with a very tasteful and powerful edge that makes me feel safe with tartan and not want to *cringe*.

WEAVER – ARAMINTA CAMPBELL

The outdoors have always played a massive part in Araminta Campbell's life. Hailing from Aberdeenshire, she was born on a small estate close to the River Dee. Her childhood sounds idyllic; exploring the fields and woods around her home nurtured her love of nature from a young age. Her wardrobe from those days – classically durable tweeds and striking tartans – shows how well dressed she's always been. Is it something in her genes, perhaps?

Araminta admits her love of art was the only thing that really overshadowed her love of the Scottish countryside. Never far from sketchbook and pencils, while her family pursued their country sporting activities, she was more inclined to visit art galleries, feeding her passion for colour and texture. After being introduced to textiles at secondary school, she discovered she had a passion for working with fabrics and followed this passion to art college to study Fine Art Embroidery.

In the final weeks of her degree, weaving struck a chord and captured Araminta's imagination. She was spurred on to find out as much as she could about weaving and its associated techniques. From here on, she taught herself. Using books, online tutorials and learning from friends, she gathered a rudimentary knowledge of the craft. Her thirst for technical skills and her artistic flair, matched with a love of colour and texture, drove her to become a highly talented weaver.

In 2014, Araminta founded her self-titled company, built around her love of craftsmanship, nature and art. Finding further inspiration in Scotland's heritage, she has created unique cloth from the word go. Over the last five years, she has gained international respect and recognition for her attention to detail and the quality of her craft. Always absorbed in the design process, she likes to be involved at every stage of a weave.

Araminta's lack of materialism is refreshing. With the heart of an artist, she sees purity and energy in all aspects of nature, and this is reflected in her design and craft. The textures she seeks tend to have a refined dimension, twinned with a hint of luxury, giving a sumptuous, tactile nature to her finished products. It's hard not to be excited by her passion for the loom, and for what it can produce.

I can't help feeling there is a truly complex, mathematical brain working away behind Araminta's artistic demeanour. There is not only talent but also a deep understanding of the mechanics of weaving behind the way she challenges the conventions and restrictions of traditional techniques. I find it wondrous how she takes pride in and time over the smallest details, such as creating a beautifully finished selvedge. I knew that distracting her from her shuttles long enough for me to delve deeper into her work would be tricky, but I managed it!

Q&A: ARAMINTA CAMPBELL

Vixy Rae: Who or what is your biggest influence or inspiration?
Araminta Campbell: A textiles teacher first opened my eyes to the creative potential in cloth and my passion grew as I studied and began creating my own fabrics. Growing up on a small estate, tweed, tartan and the Scottish landscape had always been a big part my life, but I hadn't understood how they were all interconnected. Once I saw how the natural landscapes I loved could be translated into a woven cloth, I was hooked. The Scottish landscape remains my greatest inspiration, and I describe my designs as woven paintings because they are my way of capturing the world I see around me.

Can you remember the first cloth you ever wove? What was your first commission as a professional weaver?
I started out hand-weaving small art pieces, combining yarns I had dyed using natural

plant dyes with feathers, twigs, strips of silk and embroidery. The first project I took on was creating a tapestry to represent the UK at the International Triennial of Tapestry in Łódź, Poland. This large wall hanging was handwoven from naturally dyed yarns and organic materials and told the story of the landscape through the changing seasons. Because of this tapestry I had to buy the first of the hand-weaving looms we still use here in the studio, and an individual who noticed it at an exhibition became my first ever client for a bespoke tweed design.

You are the first in a new era of artisan weavers. Are people attracted more to the ideas of tradition or to the new perspective your work provides?

I think it's a combination of the two; I believe the best designers and craftspeople are simply developing fresh ways of doing a very old thing. Respect and appreciation for the past give new work depth and

authenticity, and here in Scotland we have such a rich textile history to draw from. We can be creative, dynamic and inspiring in how we carry these traditions forward and continue innovating and learning so they remain appealing for future generations.

What sort of looms do you use?

Our two hand-weaving looms are floor dobby sample looms made by a gentleman named George Wood. He was originally a ship engineer, and then became a loom maker in Leicester around the mid-20th century. Each of his looms is a work of art in itself, custom made for each weaver. They are all individually numbered; it's estimated he made around 300 in his lifetime.

Our first loom is number 151 – with 24 shafts – and the second is number 297 – 16 shafts – which was made in 1985, when he was in his eighties! They are considered the Rolls-Royce of the loom world and I feel very privileged to have two here in our

Edinburgh studio, and to be weaving with them all these years later.

For our bespoke tartan and tweed projects, we partner with hand-picked weaving mills across Scotland. Many have looms and other machines over one hundred years old, still very much in use. These are mixed in with newer technology, so you may have the first stage of a design being managed from a computer, followed by the warp being hand-threaded onto a Victorian power loom, then the woven cloth being washed using machines from the 1960s or 1970s. It's fascinating to see all the different layers of innovation in manufacturing and, sometimes despite technological advancements, the old ways are the best!

You are building a reputation in Scotland and across the Atlantic. Who are your customers and how do they find you?
We have a diverse range of customers using our bespoke tweed and tartan service, including hotels, Savile Row tailors and family groups. With our other collections, we work with retailers like Studio Four in New York and interior designers, as well as private clients purchasing a favourite new scarf or special gift.

My customers share a desire for textiles that are more than a product, looking for items with a sense of story and provenance. They engage in the process of how their pieces are created, from the initial design and inspiration, to the materials and craftsmanship used to make them.

Customers find us through online channels, but many come through word of mouth. Because of the story behind a design and a client's connection with the process, every item has the potential to spark a conversation. This is the most powerful way of reaching an audience.

We know you have a passion for tweed, but what tartans do you favour and what new setts have you designed recently?
The tartans I'm drawn to tend to be the ancient and muted variations as these are more closely linked to colours seen in the landscape and to the naturally dyed yarns that would have been used in the past. These variations tend to sit better alongside tweeds, and I'm encountering more and more clients who wish to create a custom tweed and tartan that go well together.

The tartan I designed for the Fife Arms Hotel in Braemar is one of my favourites. I drew inspiration for the sett from the Duke of Fife Tartan, to reference the hotel's founder, and used the countryside of Royal Deeside to inform the colours. The fresh pine and moss greens are offset by deep iron-oxide red, the pink grey of the famous Grampian granite and a flash of gorse yellow. It was designed to complement the Fife Arms tweed yet still have its own strength and integrity. I'm really pleased with the result.

Weavers often have their own palette which inspires them. Can you describe your colour palette when it comes to creating cloth?
As you may have gathered, natural tones are

the basis for my aesthetic and I tend to avoid colours that look harsh or acidic. However, that doesn't prevent me from creating tartans that have real depth and intensity. Nature is full of wonderfully rich colours; it is all about getting the tone and balance right.

I pay attention to how each colour will react once it is woven. The beautiful thing about a tartan is that you will get areas of solid colour and others where the warp and weft mix two colours together, creating a blend of the two. I take into account colour theory and how the placement of colours alongside each other can change how we see them and suddenly a six-colour tartan has endless possibilities. I focus on seeing the design as a whole; the sett, the yarn colours and how they interact as they are combined in the woven cloth.

Do you believe the story behind the cloth is as important as the cloth itself?

Yes! Ultimately those who wear tartan do so because it means something to them. Whether it is a family name, military association or because it reminds them of a special place, there is an emotional connection that goes beyond its use as a cloth. I think people are increasingly interested in how a design developed and in knowing where and how the cloth has been made, which all tie into its story too.

Do you have a favourite tartan and sett design?

I grew up with the Campbell tartan and have always worn it. I love the way it has a longer repeat than you would expect, with alternating single and double tramlines. I'm married now, so wear the Stewart tartan but still enjoy that visible connection to the Campbells in my wardrobe.

As a clothing designer my garments start with the fabric, but does the fabric start with the colours, yarns, texture or pattern?

For me a design always starts with the story. As I develop a concept from my initial inspiration, this translates into the colours, textures and patterns I create. However, right from the very start, these are also linked to the yarns I will use in the cloth. This is vital as it means a completed design can be woven as it appears, rather than creating a design using digital colours that aren't actually available as yarns.

DRESSMAKER – HOLLY MITCHELL

It is refreshing to find home-grown talent who not only design but also create stylish and unique pieces from start to finish. Totty Rocks is a womenswear fashion label and boutique for independent-thinking women. Situated close to the green space of the Meadows in the stylish Bruntsfield area of Edinburgh, business partners Holly Mitchell and Lynsey Miller have forged a beautiful niche, supplying their signature pieces to both local and international clientele.

Classic ideas with a contemporary twist seem to be nothing new these days, but when you add in an element of personal flair and some edgy pattern cutting, you have a recipe for something both individual and beyond fashion. Totty Rocks' signature style is inspired by femininity, quality and an acute awareness and understanding of the female frame. Fashion forward? Perhaps, but the fact is that timeless elegance is never out of style.

Holly is the creative and practical genius behind the label, with her creations much sought-after by clients from celebrities to political powerhouses. Her sense of pride and attention to detail has moved the label forward, reinforcing it as one of the most credible Scottish independent clothing brands of recent years. Holly's love of vintage, colour and texture can be seen throughout her catalogue, with tartan always in there somewhere.

Her use of tartan is wonderfully varied, encompassing everything from the soft structure of a tartan pussy-bow blouse, to the more dramatic lines of a bias-panelled heavily tailored tartan riding coat. Silhouettes borrowed from the heroines of the golden age of Hollywood translate well into her collared tartan evening jacket with a raised sleeve head, or her cropped bias-cut bolero jacket with peaked shoulders.

Colour plays a major role in the label's seasonal offerings, with the exploration of colour dramatised in Holly's use of tartan – from the vibrant yellow and black of the Cornish tartan to the passionate reds of the MacQueen and the heather and moss tones of the Isle of Skye tartans. I managed to prise Holly away from her shears for a chat about her inspirations and aspirations.

Q&A: HOLLY MITCHELL

Vixy Rae: Which era most inspires your creations?
Holly Mitchell: We love a strong shoulder at Totty Rocks so we are always inspired by the silhouette of the 1940s. We also love the precise tailoring, incredible detailing and whimsical prints of that era.

Have you always felt a passion for clothing and design, or did it develop later in life?
My passion for clothes and fashion has been with me from as early as I can remember. I have dreamy fond memories of my mother collecting, lovingly repairing and selling the most beautiful vintage clothes when I was a child – this was and still is her occupation. I remember a 1930s tartan ball dress hanging in our sitting room which, in a way, must have influenced my love of tartan as a fashion fabric from such a young age.

Did you have formal training in pattern cutting or are you self-taught?
Both Lynsey [Miller] and I studied fashion design at Edinburgh College of Art where we both learned pattern cutting and gained BA Hons and PgDips in fashion design.

Are you more driven by the client or by the sett and colour of the tartan you'd like to use?
In our designs, we are ultimately driven by the sett and colours of each tartan, and the mood and energy they evoke.

Which of your clients is the one who has pushed you out of your comfort zone?
I'd say working with all our clients as individuals has removed any comfort zone we ever had. We put a lot of energy, care and attention into each person and their particular needs, but I'd say working with the First Minister of Scotland, Nicola Sturgeon, has been the most challenging: enjoyable but challenging. Mainly because of TV appearances, very tight deadlines and the sheer importance of everything being made to the highest of standards.

Which designer – apart from you! – has used tartan to the most creative, dramatic effect?
There are so many designers who have understood the drama of tartan, but Alexander McQueen has the edge for me.

Making much of your clothing in-house must give you a great sense of pride. Do

you prefer to source locally or globally?

Sustainability is very important to us; we source from UK-based mills and suppliers 90 per cent of the time. We also use up all of our off-cut, smaller pieces of cloth for accessories and we give anything left over to schools and crafters for their own use.

Do you like your own family tartan? And have you made anything for yourself out of it?

I absolutely love my family tartans. Campbell is green and blue and has a soft appearance while MacTavish is a fabulous vibrant orange and ice blue. It's so bold. I dream of making a fabulous Totty Rocks trench coat out of it. Unfortunately I've not had the time, but it's on the wish list!

What is your earliest memory of tartan?

As mentioned, I do remember this beautiful 1930s ball dress, but more importantly my mum made me a tartan high-waisted mini skirt for my school disco when I was twelve and I wore it with a polo neck and Doc Martens. Very '90s!

Out of all the tartan pieces you have created which has been your favourite? And why?

I made a fabulous red-and-black tartan dress for one of our most colourful customers for fashion week this year. It was a sweetheart pencil dress, cut on the bias and combined patent black leather and black Chantilly lace, but the icing on the cake was the abundance of tartan ruffles

all up the back. It had a modern punk yet feminine and sexy edge. I loved using such a variety of fabrics and techniques together on the one garment. It's something we love at Totty Rocks, how the mood of tartan can be completely changed by bias cutting or combining with leather, lace, velvet or fur.

Worst tartan mistake ever?

Trump Tartan. And let's leave it there!

DESIGNER – JUDY R. CLARK

When *Vogue* tipped Judy R. Clark as one of Britain's up and coming new talents they weren't wrong. Since her graduation, Judy has forged a respected, credible niche in the world of high-end designer ladies' fashion. With her fabulous sense of eccentricity matched with her skill in tailoring, her creations are not only breathtakingly beautiful but also wonderfully sustainable.

Having worked with many larger companies over the past few years creating installations, bespoke pieces, ranges and exhibitions, Judy is certainly a busy lady. She won Best New Scottish Designer at the Scottish Variety Awards 2012 and Womenswear Designer of the Year at the Scottish Style Awards 2013. She has worked with individuals such as Emeli Sandé and has collaborated on projects with Timorous Beasties, MYB Lace, Harris Tweed Hebrides

and Calzeat, adding a touch of flair to their designs. Judy also continues to consult and work with clients including Levi's, Ford and Nespresso, and her cutting-edge approach brought her work with the Missoni Hotel when it briefly came to Edinburgh. One of her career highlights was exploring her love for the darker, theatrical side of fashion when she interned for the late Alexander McQueen in London.

2019 was a great year for Judy. February saw her launch her 'Ready to Wear' collection at Milan Fashion Week, placing her on the global fashion stage as a leading force in British high fashion. The Ready to Wear collection combines texture and pattern in the subtlest ways, using Scottish tartan, Scottish Lace and Scottish tweed – now that really is flying the flag! Titled 'Regency' and 'Victoriana', the pieces have dramatic and theatrical silhouettes, reminiscent of a lost age of formality. With Judy's sleek tailored cuts combined with sultry lace, soft tweeds and striking tartan, the pieces have a dark and sexy edge. She has a wonderful ability to combine darkness with hints of colour and texture in panels and detailing. *Vogue Italia*'s cultural editor, upon visiting Judy's Edinburgh studio, heralded her work as 'Romantic Art'.

My favourite of her tartan pieces is the Sherlock coat; it would certainly suit Irene Adler, Sherlock Holmes's love interest. Using the regime of panelled tailoring from a tailcoat, and tailoring's rule of thirds, Judy has created a textured and sumptuous dress coat with a lifted and draped pleated front and panelled tartan back tail. The slightly exaggerated lines give a dramatic yet romantic twist.

Q&A: JUDY R. CLARK

Vixy Rae: As a Scottish designer born and bred, how important is tartan to you in your creations?
Judy R. Clark: Tartan naturally came into my work when working alongside the Scottish textile mills and in particular Calzeat in the Scottish Borders. I visited the mill on a regular basis and was fascinated by the technology they have to produce new fabric design. The fabric has such depth and history, it's one that became prominent in my work.

Were you inspired from an early age to design and create? Was it in your DNA?
I remember sitting around my parents' kitchen table drawing and painting with my sisters. I was at my happiest when I was creating, and this has stayed with me. Both my grandfathers were very creative; it's definitely something that runs in the family. My twin sister is an artist and we are always in and out of each other's studio critiquing one another and getting creative together. We designed a collection of 'art coats', featuring Christine's drawings in the linings of the coats, which was great fun to work on.

My love of clothing design in particular came when I was around fifteen. I started designing shoes and then moved on to clothes. I always had a love of life drawing, which then transformed into fashion illustration and, in turn, clothing design.

There is a fine line between stylish tartan and tartan tat. What forms the boundary?
Crisp style and quality cloth. Tailoring and design aesthetic is everything.

Which designer of the past fifty years has done the most to reinforce tartan as a credible global fabric?
Both Westwood and McQueen helped to establish tartan as an iconic fabric that was seen on a global scale. The 1970s really paved the way for the cloth during the punk era.

Tartan was originally and predominantly worn by men. Has there been a shift towards it being more accepted in the female wardrobe?
Absolutely. It's no longer a fabric just associated with men – apart from the kilt, obviously.

In the world of celebrity, who do you think wears tartan well?
The iconic photos of Naomi Campbell dressed in Vivienne Westwood will always spring to mind as well as Sarah Jessica Parker at the Met Ball with [Alexander] Lee McQueen. Rita Ora's skin-tight tartan suit was a statement outfit which she wore so well.

Mixing tartan: is it fashion design or fashion mistake?
Mixing tartans is definitely design in my book. I love to mix colours and patterns – it's one of the most exciting parts of the job. The palette of fabrics – checks, stripes, tartans, florals – mixed in the correct way can produce truly beautiful results.

What tartan is in your current wardrobe?
The Regency frock coat from my RTW collection is my go-to coat. It features MacDonald and Robertson tartan. My husband's kilt is a Douglas tartan; his grandmother gave it to him on his 21st birthday and he wore it at our wedding.

How would you describe your creative design style – does it change season to season or do you have signature themes?
My pieces are not season focused. Instead they permeate around inspiration taken from my travels or from a certain iconic piece or collection. I'm inspired by historical design and love to combine it with new fabrics. There is a certain British eccentricity about them. I do love a bustled coat and will always have a fondness for Harris Tweed.

What is your family tartan? Have you ever designed a tartan from scratch for yourself or a client?
My family tartan is Clark. My RTW collection features both the Robertson and MacDonald tartan; they were chosen to represent both my grandmothers. I was commissioned by Prestwick Airport to design a new tartan for their rebrand in 2018. I worked with their new brand colours, creating a tartan for the airport and staff uniform.

CRAFT

TARTAN

Stewart Christie Weathered

Rep rv green
Rep black
Rep blue
Old gold

IT'S ABOUT TIME

After all my delving into the myth and history of tartan I found myself wanting to get involved with the whole tartan 'cause'. My own tartan is MacRae, which my son, to my utter delight requested for his first kilt on his eighteenth birthday. Being a colourist and someone who loves to create, I wanted to see and understand the process on a personal level. All I needed was a reason. What could be better than to look back to look forward and create something with reason, conviction, heart and soul.

It seemed only natural going into the 300th year of Stewart Christie & Co., to

create something that celebrates and commemorates this historic anniversary. For once I was going to work ahead and have something ready.

Stewart Christie is the oldest bespoke tailors in Scotland, and the second oldest business in Edinburgh. I'm not sure whether the latter is actually true, but in case you were wondering the oldest is the Sheep Heid Inn in Duddingston, which was granted a licence in 1360.

Back in the early 1700s, Stewart Christie was set up under the name of Marshall Aitken with premises near North Bridge and then, as the firm grew, they took on a shop on the High Street, opposite St Giles' Cathedral. Back then, the firm was classed as cloth merchants, hosiers, shirt makers and tailors, quite the industrious enterprise of its day.

Later, the companies of J. Stewart & Co., and J. Christie & Co. were established in 1800 and 1804 respectively. John Stewart and John Christie had both been trained by Marshall Aitken, and kept closes ties with the firm. In 1933 the two firms amalgamated into Stewart, Christie & Co. A few years later they took the decision to join with Marshall Aitken. As Stewart, Christie & Co. had gained the Royal Warrant to King George V, it was decided the three businesses should operate under Stewart, Christie & Co. not Marshall Aitken. However, when the king died, the Royal Warrant was lost. Even so, as a company it has outlasted monarchs, governments and fashions trends; indeed, it's older than some countries.

A TRICENTENARY CELEBRATION

With the company's official birthday being 1720, we decided to create something for our tricentennial year. A lively debate followed: should it be a tweed, a whisky or a fragrance?

But the answer was quite obvious. We should design a Stewart Christie Tartan.

We looked through the archive to see if any previous attempts lurked there, although my thinking was perhaps in the past it was not the done thing to create one's own tartan. What we did find was was even more interesting. I spoke of the Christie tartan earlier, and we were pretty sure this was a genuinely old swatch. Peter MacDonald, the tartan historian, visited to look over our archive books, which were completed in 1885. As he flicked through, he stopped at the Christie tartan, commenting that it was possibly the oldest tartan in all the books we owned. From the yarn's coarseness and the way the colours had aged, he dated it at around 1730.

A FRESH TAKE ON THE CHRISTIE TARTAN

The Christie tartan was one idea, but I couldn't help feeling the Stewart tartan had a more regal ancestry and the proportions of the thread count a slightly more delicate feel to them. This genteel aspect gave me the feeling we could create something which would appeal to men and women alike. Then I looked more closely through the top checks and realised that the base for both tartans was the actually the Rob Roy tartan.

I spoke with Dawn Robson-Bell, head of design at Lochcarron, the famed Borders tartan mill, about all the options. Together we sought out colours which would be sympathetic to a contemporary eye. The colours of the Black Watch tartan are always a good starting point, but the danger was we might end up creating something which echoed, and could be mistaken for, a regimental tartan.

We were starting to have square eyes from looking at so many designs, and so we stepped away and revisited on a number of

occasions before we came even close to choosing the base for the cloth.

The addition of three golden stripes was essential as an echo of the three hundred years, but still we needed to work out how to show the company's evolution over time. Our ideas needed to represent balance and to illustrate the transition between the old look of the company and the new re-imagined vision of Stewart Christie as a brand in its own right. We were trying to create a tartan with its own neutrality and appeal, but with a strong defined edge to it, too.

A SECOND INCARNATION

The first printouts of our new 'modern' variant were interesting; the effect of taking the base of the navy and green from the traditional Black Watch and then interjecting the overcheck was pleasant. However, as expected, there was too much contrast between the foreground and the background, and it did have quite a serious masculine vibe to it, which lacked that essential balance we were seeking. We then asked for a second variant to be created, using more earthy and neutral tones.

The debate that followed was: should we call it ancient or weathered? At first sight, the answer was definitely weathered.

After all my ideas about creating something which would be easy to wear in the evening, this second incarnation of the design was incredibly pleasing to look at. The threads were closer to my beloved tweed yarns, and the overall effect was more relaxed and less 'sudden'. I could see that cloth in a million different settings; it felt like the story of the Hawick tartan – you just know at first glance that it's the right one.

My sense was that the tricky bit would be to persuade everyone else, but to my utter amazement the response from all those directly involved in Stewart Christie was the same. We were to . . .

'WEAVE IT!'

The only issue now is that we need to go back to the drawing board and create at least another two variants. That will certainly mean a lot more fun for me!

"

I suppose in some way we are all like tartan, created from the same yarn, but not woven on the same loom to the same sett. All of us individuals but having similar colours running through us; perhaps that's why tartan is a cloth of people rather than place.

VIXY RAE

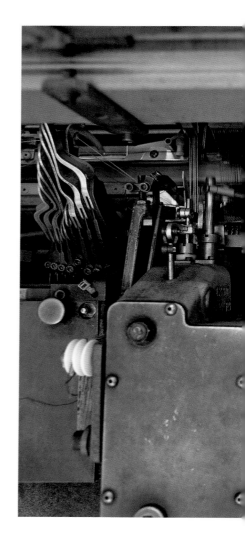

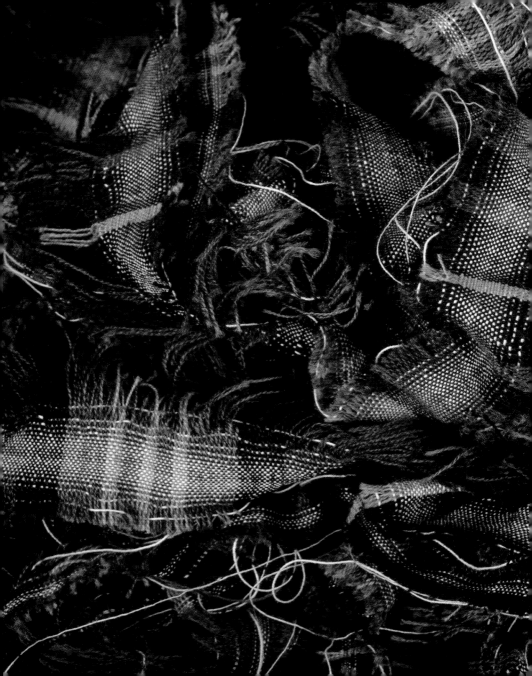

BEYOND

TARTAN
Sartorial Portraits

A TARTAN FUTURE

So, what is the future for tartan? Calling a tartan truly Scottish is like calling pizza Italian. It has a strong grounding in and association with the country whence it came, and the stories around it are still of this place, but it is created and sold the world over, and is consumed and enjoyed in many different forms.

Tartan is distilled in myth and romance, flamboyance and rebellion, surrounded by lies and kept alive by a glorious truth. Globally, it is seen as Scottish no matter where it is produced or sold. My own journey through the history of the fabric has delved into its secret lives to give me an insight into and perspective on how the cloth has been promoted and received, used and abused, over the centuries. My opinion has shifted from one of slight distaste to one of intrigue. I understand tartan's place in history and its tradition, but I also see that it has been commandeered to spin length after length of myth and romantic fiction from historical fact.

AN EMBROIDERED STORY

Heralding from a time when truths and stories were seldom written but instead handed down from one age to the next by word of mouth, it is easy to see how the history of tartan has become embroidered and fabricated. Formal records emerged with the Industrial Revolution, but even then they were based on romanticised ideals of tartan. This era ushered in the industrial age of weaving; it was now possible to produce tartan with consistency both in terms of quality and colour, thanks to chemical dyes.

INDUSTRIAL QUANTITIES

The Industrial Revolution was instrumental in the birth of modern tartan. Those looking to reinforce the heritage of the cloth and benefit from large-scale weaving used folklore and myth to promote tartan and increase its popularity. Scotland was ready to believe whole-heartedly in the very fabric of its identity, and so the stage was set and the past – at least in some cases – rewritten. In less than one hundred years, the 54 clan tartans recorded in Logan's Scottish Gael of 1831 and the unreliable yet impactful *Vestiarium Scoticum* of 1842 had nearly doubled as Scotland embraced its iconic cloth. These texts, alongside Mclan's *Clans of the Scottish Highlands*, went a long way towards embedding the idea of clan tartan within Scotland.

From these, perhaps less than humble, beginnings, the foundations of tartan were laid. It was then up to different people to build upon these notions and integrate tartan into all the meanings of Scottish identity. Families began to add and create their 'sept', or stake their claims to be rightful wearers of the cloth. Inevitably this became a 'fashion', and helped power a need to be recognised as someone of noble blood or of true Scottish ancestry.

Inevitably, tartan would either flourish or simply fade away. But when a nation and a people support an idea, it seems natural that it would become embedded in history, built upon and diversified to reflect the world as it changes. Today there are thousands of tartans, from individuals, families, societies, locations, companies and nations, with colour and sett each forming inexhaustible, unique combinations of personality and taste. Perhaps it shows that, although we are all created from the same yarn, we are woven on different looms. Our sett is our experiences, the colour our character.

THE CHOICE IS YOURS

Tartan is a bold, unshakeable, resonant statement of Scottishness; it echoes with pride, unity, passion, rebellion. It just depends how, and if, you choose to wear it.

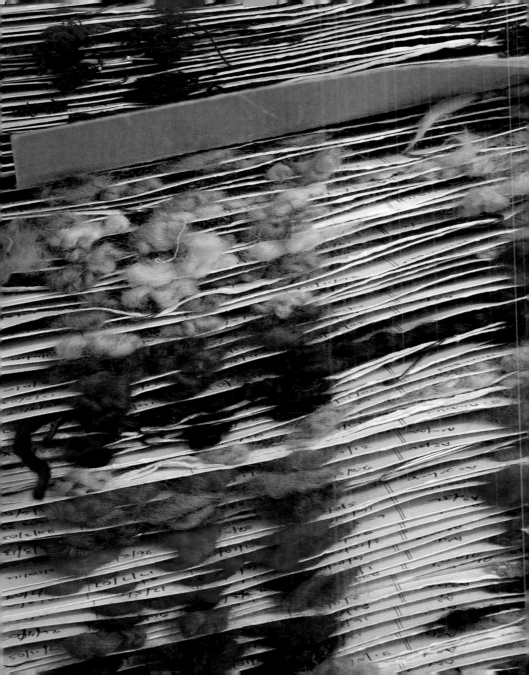

FURTHER READING

Anderson, L. (2004) *Braveheart: From Hollywood to Holyrood*, Luath Press

Anstey, H. and Weston T. (1997) *Guide to Textile Terms*, Weston Publishing

Bain, R. (1953) *The Clans and Tartans of Scotland*, Collins, 1976 edn

Baker, K. (2005) *George IV: A Life in Caricature*, Thames and Hudson

Barthes, R. (1967) *The Fashion System*, University California Press, 1990 edn

Bolton, A. (2003) *Men in Skirts*, V&A Publications

Breward, C. (2003) *Fashion*, Oxford University Press

Cannizzo, J. (2005) *Our Highland Home: Victoria and Albert in Scotland*, National Galleries of Scotland

Carter, M. (2003) *Fashion Classics: From Carlyle to Bathes*, Berg

Cheape, H. (1991) *Tartan: The Highland Habit*, National Museums of Scotland

Cosgrave, B. (2005) *Sample: 100 Fashion Designers*, Phaidon

Davies, R. (1970) *Fifth Business*, W. H. Allen & Co, 1977 edn

Dunbar, J.T. (1962) *History of Highland Dress*, Oliver & Boyd, 1983 edn

Ewing, E. (1977) *History of Children's Costume*, Bibliophile, 1986 edn

Faiers, J. (2008) *Tartan*, Berg

Foden, G. (1998) *The Last King of Scotland*, Faber & Faber

Foreman, C. (2004) *Made in Scotland: Household Names That Began in Scotland*, Birlinn

Gow, I. (1992) *The Scottish Interior*, Edinburgh University Press

Grant, I. F. (1996) *Highland Folk Ways*, Birlinn, 1995 edn

Grimble, I. (2004) *Scottish Clans and Tartans*, Octopus

Innes of Learney, Sir T. (1938) *The Tartans of the Clans and Families of Scotland*, Johnson and Bacon, 1964 edn

Lurie, A. (1981) *The Language of Clothes*, Random House Inc.

Mackie, J. D. (1982) *A History of Scotland*, Penguin

Maclean, F. (1987) *Highlanders: A History of the Highland Clans*, David Campbell, 2000 edn

McArthur, C. (2003) *Braveheart, Brigadoon and the Scots: Distortions of Scotland in Hollywood Cinema*, I. B. Tauris

McDermott, C. (2002) *Made in Britain: Tradition and Style in Contemporary British Fashion*, Mitchell Beazley.

McDowell, C. (2001) *Ralph Lauren: the Man, the Vision, the Style*, Castell Illustrated

Polhemus, T. and L. Procter (1978) *Fashion & Anti-fashion*, Thames & Hudson

Riberio, A. (1986) *Dress and Morality*, Batsford

Rose, J. (2001) *The Intellectual Life of the British Working Classes*, Yale Nota Bene

Rothestein, N. (1984) *Four Hundred Years of Fashion*, V&A Publications

Scarlett, J. D. (1990) *Tartan: The Highland Textile*, Shepheard-Walwyn

Stewart, D. C. (1950) *The Setts of the Scottish Tartans*, Shepheard-Walwyn, 1974 edn

Stewart, D. W. (1893) *Old & Rare Scottish Tartans*, George P. Johnston

Teal of Teallach, G. and P. D. Smith (1992) *District Tartans*, Shepheard-Walwyn

Tower, J. and Levitt C. (1984) *Fabric of Society: A Century of People and Their Clothes*, Laura Ashley Publications

Way, G. and, R. Squire (2000) *Clan and Tartans*, HarperCollins

Wilcox, C. (2005) *Vivienne Westwood*, V&A Publications

Zaczek, I. and C. Phillips (2004) *The Complete Book of Tartan*, Hermes House

Plus, the internet, customers, friends and historians.

IMAGE CREDITS

All photography except images credited below © Stewart Christie & Co.

viii Eric Musgrave

x, 35(left), 52, 120, 153, 154, 192(top), 194, 202(right), 224, 243, 245, 259, 261, 275, 276, 279, 280-85, 292 Laura Meek

2, 3, 9, 13, 15, 20, 21, 30, 41, 42, 51, 62(bottom), 67, 70, 78, 99, 119, 124, 125, 129, 151, 152, 161, 163, 166-69, 173, 178, 181, 191, 201, 208, 219, 220, 229, 231-37, 241, 242, 249, 251, 267 Laura Meek(photo)/Stewart Christie & Co(styled)

10, 24, 38, 47, 63, 77, 95, 96, 142, 160, 197, 214, 227, 238 Vixy Rae

11, 223 National Museums Scotland

16(top left), 56, 68 The Scottish Tartans Authority

16(top right) 7th Duke Atholl Günter Josef Radig

16(bottom left), 22(right), 23 Lady Ann Dunmore

27 Laura Meek/Daniel Fearn(styling)

33, 39, 93, 94, 97, 105, 107-117, 126, 134, 137, 140, 159, 258, 268-73, 287 Alix McIntosh

35(right), 74, 130, 174-177, 184, 187, 189, 198(top), 225 Laura Meek(photo)/Stewart Christie & Co

48(left) John McLeish

59-61 Sigma Films/David Eustace(photo)

62(top) Duncan McGlynn

81-92 Alix McIntosh/Vixy Rae(styling)

69, 155, 156 Lochcarron of Scotland

104 Robin Elliot

106(bottom) Jane Barlow/PA Archive/PA Images

144 Laura Meek(photo)/James Marchant-Wink(model)/Stewart Christie & Co(styled)

145 Laura Meek(photo)/Julian MacDonald(model)/Stewart Christie & Co(styled)

146 Laura Meek (photo)/Tabitha Edith Stevens(model)/Stewart Christie & Co(styled)

147 Laura Meek(photo)/Michael Maclean (model)/Stewart Christie & Co(styled)

149(top) Laura Meek(photo)/James McCallum(model)/Stewart Christie & Co(styled)

149(bottom) Laura Meek(photo)/Kyle Jamieson(model)/Stewart Christie & Co(styled)

164, 165 Fats Shariff

170 Laura Meek(photo)/Simone Murphy(model)/Stewart Christie & Co(styling)

THANK YOU

My wonderful business partner Daniel Fearn, who has helped me not only grow up over the years, but also in my research throughout this project and by putting up with me daily and giving me the time and space to be myself always and write this book. A true gentleman by nature and a valued friend.

I couldn't be more grateful for the friends in my life, especially the people I've been lucky enough to work with on this creative journey; without them I could never have pushed myself this far.

Laura Meek, Alix McIntosh, David Eustace for their beautiful photography.

My editor Emma Hargrave, my assistant Tabitha Stevens.

Plus, Eric Musgrave, Gordon Millar, John McLeish, Sam Heughan, Alexander McCall Smith, John Byrne, Robin Deas, Clare Campbell, Dawn Robson-Bell, Lesley Penny, Emily Martin, Peter MacDonald, Roddy Riddell, Ronnie Proctor, Robin Elliot, Lady Dunmore, David Mackenzie, Araminta Campbell, Holly Mitchell, Judy R. Clark, Rosie Waine, Jamie Macnab, Stewart Christie & Co., Black & White Publishing, Custom Lane, Scottish Tartans Authority . . .

A huge thanks to all of you!

ABOUT THE AUTHOR

Before Vixy Rae took over Stewart Christie & Co. this Edinburgh institution was run by four generations of men named Duncan Lowe. Stewart Christie prides itself on garments of such quality and appeal that they last for decades. Vixy is the first female member of the Incorporation of Edinburgh Tailors, a trade body which dates back more than six centuries.

Vixy with her son, Saul.